Acknowledgment

It has been said that behind every successful man is a woman. Along my road to success are many ladies who deserve that distinction. Their never ending support has made my life one I'm proud of. They are: my mother, Louise Rowe, who has always been there when needed; my daughter, Stephanie, and her mother, Carole, who played important roles in many of the stories herein; my step-daughter, Andrea, who trained my favorite horse, Walter; my wife, Janet, whose encouragement resulted in this book; Janie Harrison, my literary expert in Mannheim, Germany; and Toni Cunningham who designed the cover and assisted me weekly. There is a special man that I must mention, last but not least, my deceased father John Rowe. He and I shared many special times together; he loved animals as much as I.

Introduction

This book is a series of short stories about animals. They are all true experiences, occurring over a twenty-five year time frame. I have been described as the man who likes animals more than people. To an extent this is true; I have an ability to relate with animals which, I believe, is a gift from above. The loyalty of a pet to his owner is unparalleled in today's society. The happenings you will read about, some published in newspapers, dog journals and seen on television, clearly illustrate the incredible intelligence level of dogs, cats, and horses.

With a background in aviation, I am a total skeptic. Things either work or they don't. Theories must be proven to me before acceptance. My profession for thirty years flying airliners demanded perfection, with thousands of human lives depending on my ability and proficiency. I was never allowed to go to work and practice. Some of these incidents were so incredible that if they had not occurred to me I would have difficulty believing them. Imagine Midnight, the cat, returning after a two year absence. Visualize Tiny Gooney's eye lost in a fight and its regeneration. Think about Walter, the horse, seeking help after being bitten by a rattlesnake.

I am convinced that animals have the

ability to think, reason, and make judgments. They can discern right from wrong and many possess a large vocabulary which they understand. Our animals are a product of their environment just as our children are.

I have devoted fifteen years of research to animal nutrition. This book is an effort to inform owners why so many animals are sick, and die while still in their prime of life.

Dedication

This book is dedicated to Hank, the most unique dog I have known. He was my constant companion until his untimely death May 29, 1996. I look for him each day.

Table of Contents

Chapter One

**KNOW WHAT YOU'RE FEEDING YOUR DOG;
I DIDN'T AND SHE DIED.**

Lizzy

My interest in animal nutrition began with the death of a special dog; this is her story. In the late 1970's I trained bird dogs on a ranch near Brady, Texas. A good friend informed me about a special dog he had hunted behind. He told me this English Setter, who was white and black ticked, was a superb bird finder. When it was hot and windy, she would find birds. Even when it was raining, she would point the elusive Bob White Quail. She belonged to a gentleman in Oklahoma with failing health and was for sale. I phoned the owner and purchased her sight unseen.

I made arrangements to pick her up on my way to New Mexico where I had plans to hunt pheasant and quail with my friends, the

Robertsons on their Ione Ranch. At that time I flew a Cessna 182, single engine aircraft to my various bird leases and hunting trips. The back seat belonged to my dogs who always enjoyed the ride.

Upon arrival at a small airport in Oklahoma, the owner had a friend there to meet us with the setter. Her owner was so fond of her he couldn't bear to watch his six year old companion disappear into the sky.

As I approached "Liz," she began to curl her lips, showing her pearly whites. Lizzy was a "grinner." She hopped into the back seat of the airplane without any help, as if she knew exactly what was happening.

A pilot friend of mine was accompanying me on the trip. I would be landing on a grass strip near Nara Visa, New Mexico. I decided to stop and refuel at Dalhart, Texas. Dalhart is a small airport with very little air traffic. After landing I taxied to the fuel pumps, shut the engine down and opened my door. Liz jumped out of the door and was running full speed across the airport. My friend looked at me and commented, "That's the last time you'll see that dog."

I began chasing after her, blowing a whistle, shouting, and then crossing the runway. I was beginning to get worried as she was now several hundred yards distant approaching the far end of the airport. To my surprise she stopped along side of the runway and pointed. My friend had caught up by this time and said, "That dog not only runs off; she's a liar too." We approached cautiously and I was talking to her gently, hoping she would not run off again. She was so intense I gave her the benefit of the doubt and I walked in front of her kicking the weeds. Suddenly a covey of quail burst into the air just a yard in front of Liz's nose. I turned, looked back and she was still on point, looking at me and grinning, showing those teeth. I reached down and gave her a big hug. This was her way of telling me I had just purchased one hell of a bird dog.

From that day on she never let me down. It never seemed to matter what the weather was: rain, snow, hot or windy; Liz always found and pointed the birds, whether they be pheasant or quail. Many times the other dogs would run all morning and be birdless, but Liz was always able to produce at least one covey of birds.

After three great years together, Liz became sick one day. I drove her to my veterinarian who diagnosed her with liver and kidney failure. I then made an appointment with a veterinary internist. After a day of testing, his diagnosis was the same. Lizzy died the next day.

This was my introduction to animal nutrition. For, you see, it was a contributing factor in this great animal's death. The vet explained how the high protein had destroyed her kidneys, and the chemicals ruined her liver.

Until this occurrence, like most people, I

fed my animals whatever was popular or had the best price. I made sure it was always *"high protein."* Never had I taken the time to read the entire ingredients label.

At this stage I became obsessed with animal nutrition. I felt through ignorance, I was a cause of this great animal's death. I read everything I could find and began research of my own regarding pet foods. I attended pet food seminars and eventually assisted several pet food companies with research and development of **all natural** foods. I found very few pet food companies producing quality foods for our pets. The animal's well being was not their primary concern; the bottom line, profit margin was.

What I began to find was appalling: foods with ingredients no one would purchase if they knew the contents, products full of chemical preservatives; animal by-products with virtually no nutritional benefit; essential trace minerals that are difficult if not impossible, to absorb. The list of horrors goes on and on. The hardest pill to swallow was learning the Association of American Feed Control Officials allows these products in pet foods. They even admit some are harmful!

There is absolutely no reason dogs can't live to be 16-18 years of age and cats 18 years and longer. With proper nutrition and exercise our animals can live a longer and healthier life.

Chapter Two

CROCKETTS DEEP FREEZE
AND THE HIGH PROTEIN MYTH

Crockett's Deep Freeze
"Buddy"

High Protein food may hinder your dog's performance and contribute to heat prostration. In 1970 an English Setter Dog by the name of Johnny Crockett, won the most prestigious field trial in the United States. This was the National Field Trial Championship conducted on the Ames Plantation near Grand Junction, Tennessee. To win this event requires more than luck. During the three hour test the dog will cover approximately 30 miles. Competing in February there is often snow, freezing rain and muddy conditions making this trial more difficult. The winner is one with stamina and the intelligence to pace himself for three hours. He must possess bird sense, running along forest edges where he can smell, locate and point the Bob White Quail.

Above all the dog must handle, always in earshot and always listening for the handler's instructions.

The winner of this trial sets the standard for all others to follow. This title usually guarantees a retirement to stud, producing a lucrative income for the owner.

Shortly after winning this title, Johnny Crockett developed a terminal brain tumor. His owner had the forethought to collect semen and have it frozen. At that time artificial breeding with frozen semen was limited to cattle. Texas A & M University conducted the collection process and stored the semen in nitrogen tanks. There it remained for nine years. In 1980 a gentleman from Boise, Idaho with a lifelong interest in English Setters, bred a female to this frozen semen. This was the first artificial breeding of this type in the setter world. From this breeding came a young dog named *Crockett's Deep Freeze,* so named from whence he came.

During his first three years of life he was campaigned on the field trial circuit. He traveled to the prairies of Canada in the summer for training. He then competed in field trials from Canada to Florida to California. During this three years he amassed 22 wins and was then retired to stud. It was after his retirement that I acquired him and brought him to Texas.

"Buddy," as he was affectionately called, became the centerpiece and foundation for my breeding and training program. His genealogy, dating back to the 1920's, has proven to be the cornerstone for many breeders around the globe.

From the first day with me it was obvious he was not just an ordinary dog. His affection and loyalty was demonstrated time and time again. This guy could run like the wind, usually a mile to the front when I was horseback. However, when afoot quail hunting, he was always in sight just a short distance ahead. These traits can't be taught; they come from within.

When exercising my other dogs, Buddy was the leader of the road gang. Hitched in a sledding harness and attached to a four wheeler, up to eight dogs would pull for an hour. This method of conditioning has proved itself and is utilized worldwide. Some dogs would tire and have to be removed, not Buddy; he possessed unlimited stamina and desire.

Janet Roading Nik, Spike, Lil' Checkers, John, Traveler, and Checkers

Crockett's Deep Freeze was always fed a low protein food. At Crockett Kennels his diet was never more than 20% protein. During his thirteenth year he began to slow with signs of aging. I stopped his exercise routine and he spent the days underneath a hundred year old oak tree. There he watched his offspring go through their various stages of training.

One day in September of his fourteenth year, Buddy was somewhat lethargic. I was concerned and drove him to the vet. The vet looked over his medical record noticing he had never been sick before, and that he was going on 15 years of age. He then suggested he was showing signs of kidney and or liver failure. I asked him to run a blood test and told him that I did not agree with his diagnosis. The vet returned with the lab results with an astonished look on his face. He said this dog's liver and kidney function were the equivalent of a much younger dog. Further examination revealed his heart was failing.

On the morning of September 11, 1994 Buddy and I walked together to the large oak tree where he spent his days. There he and I reminisced over the years we spent together. He laid beside me and rested his bold head on my knee. He took his last breath and died peacefully. Hopefully my death will be with dignity and grace as was his. Today his sons, daughters, and their offspring share that spot under the hundred year old oak.

Buddy's statistics are impressive. He bred 126 females, who averaged 9.5 puppies per litter. He produced many gun dogs and field trial champions alike. His last breeding took place just 3 months before his death. Always he had an eye for the girls. This great animal was never sick a day in his life. I attribute his health and longevity to an **All natural low protein** diet.

Dogs and cats do not have the ability to perspire freely as humans do. Instead they pant and cool their body temperature through their tongue. **High protein** food produces heat. A high protein diet is not necessary especially in hot climates. In fact it is harmful and can bring on heat prostration quickly, and often without warning.

High protein builds muscle like a weight lifter desires. A diet of carbohydrates produces energy and stores glycogen for future use when available energy is depleted. Marathoners and other top athletes maintain a similar diet of high carbohydrates.

Would you run your furnace all summer with warm outside temperatures? This is the equivalent of feeding your dog that **high protein** pet food. Protein must be broken down by the kidneys. Needlessly overworked, these organs, essential for life, fail prematurely.

Chapter Three

UNDERSTANDING THE INGREDIENTS LABEL

An old adage says *"You're never too old to learn."* This has never been more important than with animal nutrition.

DC - 7

For thirty years I had the pleasure of flying for Delta Air Lines. My career began in the piston era. I flew the DC-6 and DC-7, 4 engine propeller planes powered by reciprocating engines. I loved these aircraft with their giant radial engines and a noise all their own. I loved the thrill of landing these giant birds so smoothly that the passengers would think they were still in the air. During night flights I could often surprise and sometimes scare the "Stewardess" as we called them back then. When climbing, the engines were run with a rich fuel mixture to aid in cooling. Once leveled off in cruise, the fuel controls were adjusted, creating a mixture to conserve fuel and run the engines more efficiently. When climbing, the exhaust of each engine emitted long steaks of flame. As the mixture was adjusted in cruise, this flame would change to several colors, an erie light show for those unaccustomed to seeing it. Many of the new gals, (there were only female stewardesses then) would get quite a thrill peeking out the window into the night's black sky to see this light show.

These powerful engines developing up to 3350 HP each had 36 cylinders with 72 sparkplugs, two per cylinder. I became so familiar with these engines and their sound, I could tell when one of the cylinders was misfiring. I felt I knew everything there was to know about these wonderful machines. I was a self proclaimed expert, and then came the jets.

The jet aircraft had engines with no pistons, cylinders or spark plugs and the oil was never changed. Swept wings with unusual flight characteristics, they could achieve speeds of 600 mph. Suddenly I realized I had a lot to learn; the times were changing and I would have to conform to continue. I did and was fortunate to fly the most advanced airliners in the world, aircraft with the technology to take off, cruise, descend, land, and then taxi to the gate controlled by computers. Aviation has progressed far beyond most of our imaginations.

Boeing 727

Unfortunately, the development of pet foods has not witnessed as much progress as seen in aviation. In fact, just the opposite is true. We all have the ability to read and understand the ingredients, and can play an important role in demanding **all natural** pet and human foods for the future.

Ingredients must be listed and labeled on all pet food bags and cans under their specific name. These ingredient names along with their respective definitions are listed in the next chapter "Pet Food Regulations" to help you understand what you are purchasing.

One of the most important sentences contained in the official publication, The Association of American Feed Control Officials', "Pet Food Regulatory Philosophy" is one I hope you will remember. It states the purpose of this association. The following quote is from Chapter four, Part One, Sub Title AAFCO Philosphy Regarding Feed Regulation.

*"A major function of feed regulation is to safeguard the health of man and animals. A list of substances acceptable as feed ingredients must be established including their designated names and definitions. Standards should be set for substances determined to be **UNSAFE IN FEED.**"*

(Bold print added by author.)

It should be evident after this quote, that there is no agency working to protect our animals. They even admit to allowing unsafe chemicals to be used in food products.

Many pet foods utilize chemical preservatives, including ethoxyquin, BHA or BHT. These preservatives are used to preserve the fat which makes the food palatable. These preservatives are the cheapest way to prevent rancidity. They also give the food a shelf life of 2 years or more. The alternative to chemical preservation is **natural preservation,** using vitamins. Vitamins or natural preservatives are more costly and the shelf life is reduced to 6-9 months. The **natural way** to preserve food is with Vitamin E or "tocopherols".

Ethoxyquin is also utilized as an ingredient in a herbicide and rubber preservative. This chemical has never been approved for use in human foods. In the January-February issue of <u>Natural Pet</u>, a conversation between the FDA and

Monsanto was revealed. Ethoxyquin was said to be both harmful and deleterious. The FDA also stated that Ethoxyquin could not be fed safely to mammals for a long period of time.

The December 1993 issue of <u>Dog World</u> listed independent laboratory research of the chemicals BHA and BHT. *Keep in mind this chemical is approved for use in human foods.* This research concerning these chemicals showed a marked increase of certain types of cancerous tumors.

What is BHA and BHT? Butylated hydroxyanisole and butylated hydroxytoluene respectively. BHA and BHT are chemical preservatives which have no place in your diet—much less the diet of your children or pets. Their only purpose is to prevent the junky hydrogenated vegetable oil in food from going rancid. The allowable level of BHA/BHT can be as high as 0.1 percent in some foods. That's an interesting percentage because it corresponds exactly to the level in the food that rats were fed in a study in Australia. The rats didn't have too much trouble—just that their hair fell out and their blood cholesterol went through the roof. Of course the baby rats born to rats who ate the same amount of BHA/BHT proportionately that you're probably eating did have some problems. They were born *without* eyes. Subsequent studies done at Loyola University in the United States confirmed these findings.

After these results the FDA finally got

around to asking companies who dope your food with BHA/BHT to please start animal tests to see if maybe these chemicals will make your wife give birth to a baby without eyes as well. Doesn't it sound a little strange that the FDA would be asking the companies to test their own product and then tell us if it's really safe? It's like the police putting an ad in the newspaper asking all criminals to report to the police station as soon as they commit a crime. Twenty-five years after everyone was convinced that cigarettes cause lung cancer, the cigarette companies are still insisting that cigarettes are safe, non-addictive and healthful.

In Britain they're a little smarter. The use of BHT in foods is forbidden—period. You don't need BHA/BHT in your foods or your pets' food. Why feed your animals these chemicals admittedly proven harmful? They can only hurt your animal's performance and shorten his/her life. **All Natural Foods** are the answer. Their cost is insignificant compared to the loss of just one animal.

Avoid any pet food that lists the words *"by-products"* or *"middlings"* of any type or kind. Most of these ingredients have little or no nutritional value. They produce excess stools which smell bad, and are the cheapest products available for pet foods. I suggest looking for products which list *"meal"* rather than *"by-products"* and various grains without *"middlings"* after it. Middlings are a by-product of grain milling. For a definition of meat by-products see Chapter Five, Part 3: Pet Food Ingredient Definitions.

I am listing a sample ingredient label from one of the **all natural pet food companies**. This particular food is specifically designed for puppies, which I feed for one full year. Some additional minerals and nutrients are added. The 27% protein is ideal for the puppies muscle development and nutritional needs. Ingredients are listed according to their respective percentage in the food. The first ingredient is the largest quantity and the last will be the least amount. Ingredients:

Chicken Meal, Ground Brown Rice, Ground Whole Wheat, Ground Yellow Corn, Poultry Fat (preserved with Mixed Tocopherols and Ascorbyl Palmitate), Rice Bran, Corn Gluten Meal, Natural Chicken Flavor, dehydrated Whole Egg, Dried Cheese, Linseed Meal, Lecithin, Brewers Dried Yeast, Salt, Choline Chloride, Potassium Chloride, Asorbic Acid (Source of Vitamin C), Calcium Carbonate, Iron Amino Acid Chelate, Yucca Schidigera Extract, Vitamin E Supplement, Zinc Amino Acid Chelate, Manganese Amino Acid Chelate, Cobalt Amino Acid Chelate, Copper Amino Acid Chelate, Biotin, Vitamin A Acetate, Calcium Pantothenat, Thiamine Mononitrate (B1), Vitamin B 12 Supplement, Niacin, Menadione Sodium Bisulfite Complex (source of Vitamin K Activity), riboflavin Supplement, Vitamin 3 Supplement, Folic Acid, DL - Methionine, Pyridoxine Hydrochloride, Sodium

Selenite, Calcium Iodate.

This food contains 27% Protein, 16% fat, 3% fiber, 10% moisture, 1.2% Calcium, 1% phosphorus.

Beginning their second year I switch to an "all natural" maintenance food. The contents will be similar with a few deletions and additions adjusting for the animals maturity. I suggest no more than 25% protein. A house dog that is basically inactive needs no more than 18-20% protein.

Many animals develop skin allergies and associated problems. Most of these can be eliminated by choosing an **all natural food** without *corn* or *wheat*. The problem has been traced to corn gluten meal and certain wheat products. By switching to a food such as lamb and rice these symptoms often disappear. *Warning:* you must read the ingredient label. Lamb and rice products are available with corn and wheat still listed as an ingredient.

AAFCO requires that all foods contain trace minerals such as copper, iron, etc. What they don't require is that these minerals be chelated for rapid absorption. Most pet foods use mineral oxides and sulfates. You can scrape a piece of iron and produce your own iron oxide from the rusty surface.

If you picked up a handful or very small pebbles and fed them to your animal, it would be the equivalent of feeding oxides and sulfates.

Our animals are not equipped to absorb these minerals unless they are in a *"chelated form"*. This process produces minerals in a powder-like substance, readily absorbed by the animal's intestinal tract.

AAFCO has feeding "protocols" for both dog and cat foods. They call them a proving of an unqualified representation of nutritional adequacy.

This testing period for new foods runs from 10 weeks for cats to 26 weeks for dogs. That's like saying if you can drink alcohol for 26 weeks, survive and not get sick, then you can drink for life with no fear of health risk. Our government agencies are ineffective figureheads at best.

The following is a list of essential nutrients and their respective function:

Protein...Muscle
Fat...............................Glycogen, Body Reserves
Polyunsaturated Oils...................Hair, Skin, Hoof
Calcium.................................Body Fluids, Bones
Copper...Blood
Cobalt...Blood
Iron...Blood
Zinc.....................................Metabolism
Phosphorus........................Metabolism, Bones
Magnesium.................................Body Fluids
Potassium...................................Body Fluids
Manganese.................................Metabolism
Iodine.....................................Thyroid
Selenium.................................Muscle

Sodium Chloride.......................................Body Fluids
Vitamin A............................Eyes, Skin, Metabolism
Vitamin B-12...........................Blood, Metabolism
Vitamin D...Bones
Vitamin E.............................Muscles, Metabolism
Vitamin K..Blood
Biotin......................................Metabolism
Niacin......................................Nerves, Metabolism
Thiamin (B1)..Enzymes
Riboflavin (B2)...................................Metabolism
Choline Chloride...............................Metabolism
PantothenicAcid..................................Metabolism
Pyridoxine (B 6)........................Blood, Metabolism

In a random selection of 29 pet foods I found nineteen (19) using chemical preservatives and eleven (11) listing by-products as a primary ingredient.

Veterinary schools do not require students to take courses in nutrition. Many pet foods sold through veterinary clinics contain chemical preservatives and by-products. I suggest you read the ingredient label before purchasing these foods.

Chapter Four

PET FOOD REGULATIONS

Part 1

AAFCO by-laws and Regualtory Philosphy

Part 2

AAFCO Feeding Protocols for dog and cat foods

Part 3

Pet food Ingredient Definitions

Part 4

Additives and GRAS (Generally Recogonized as Safe) Substances

Standards and protocols are set forth as guidelines for the pet food industry by American Feed Control Officials. Each state is responsible for the licensing of pet food products produced within that respective state.

The Association of American Feed Control Officials is comprised of an independent group of agriculture feed experts. These individuals are the heads or chiefs of experiment stations, departments of agriculture, bureaus, divisions, sections, and laboratories and employees thereof charged by law with the examination of animal feeds and livestock remedies.

This organization is funded entirely through membership fees and sales of its official publication. It is not controlled by the government or Federal Food and Drug Administration in any way.

Excerpts from the AAFCO publication explain their regulatory philosophy. Also listed are feeding protocols for dog and cat foods and ingredients definitions which will be discussed in other chapters.

Anyone interested in developing a pet food should read this entire chapter. Otherwise Part one and Part three contain the data referred to in other chapters.

These excerpts are printed by permission of Mr. Paul Bachman, current President of Association of American Feed Control Officials Incorporated. Copies of this publication can be obtained by contacting: Charles P. Frank, AAFCO Treasurer, Georgia Department of Agriculture, Plant food, Feed and Grain Division, Capitol Square, Atlanta, GA. 30334 (404) 656-3637

Price $25.00 per copy

Part 1.
AAFCO By-Laws & Regulatory Philosophy
AAFCO AND FEED REGULATION

Feed regulation has had a long, colorful and sometimes controversial history. Thanks to a few historical sketches the events of the early days of AAFCO and feed regulation have been preserved. Early commodity regulations started with laws governing weights and measures. These regulations were formulated out of a need to protect consumers and honest merchants from unfair and deceptive practices. A penalty structure was also established to act as a deterrent, with capital punishment being the extreme. Regulations governing the quality of human food were the first to be established with feed regulations following sometime later. Feed regulations changed with the times. The quality of early mixed feeds containing whole grains could easily be determined by the consumer through the use of sight, smell and sometimes taste. Later when feeds were made with ground grains the consumer could no longer determine product quality by such simple methods. The consumer then needed assistance from someone who could assure him the foodstuff met certain standards. As beneficial components such as protein and fat were discovered they soon became the yardsticks by which feeds were judged and as more nutrients were discovered they too became standards of measurement.

PURPOSE AND FUNCTION OF AAFCO

In 1909 when control officials first convened as a committee certain objectives were established. The first objective was for the control officials to be prepared to answer industry's questions with carefully considered composite opinions. Other aims included the preparation of a uniform feed bill- formulation of fair and equitable definitions, regulations, and resolutions; acceptance of new feed ingredients and establishment of proper labeling requirements. Careful consideration before acting was an established policy of the founders as they were quick to realize that until the Association had established a degree of prestige and authority it could not afford adverse publicity. Among the purposes set for itself by the young Association was the project of formulating and distributing a set of uniform definitions covering all feed ingredients, together with their proper labeling. From the start, the Association has made concerted efforts to work with industry in every way possible, while realizing their primary duty of protecting the consumer. The foundation for expressing the modern day purpose of AAFCO has already been established by control officials of the past. One of the most eloquent statements expressing the purpose of AAFCO can be found in the most basic document of the AAFCO organization, the by-laws. Support of this statement is reaffirmed by inclusion in this document as follows:

"The purpose of the corporation shall be to establish and maintain an Association through which officials of any state, dominion, federal or other governmental agency on the North American Continent, and employees thereof charged with a responsibility in enforcing the laws regulating the production, labeling, distribution, or sale of animal feeds or livestock remedies may unite to explore the problems encountered in administering such laws, to develop just and equitable standards, definitions and policies to be followed in enforcing such laws, to promote uniformity in such laws, regulations and enforcement policies, and to cooperate with members of the industry producing such products in order to promote the effectiveness and usefulness of such products."

Other expressions of purpose can also be found in the AAFCO official publication and after thoroughly considering their merit it was determined that the following is also worthy of inclusion in this document:

A basic goal of AAFCO is to provide a mechanism, for developing and implementing uniform and equitable laws, regulations, standards, definitions and enforcement policies for regulating the manufacture, labeling, distribution and sale of animal feeds; resulting in safe, effective, and useful feeds. The Association thereby promotes new ideas and innovative procedures and urges their adoption by member agencies, for uniformity."

Building from this foundation certain key elements supporting the structure of AAFCO become apparent as cornerstones of the Association. Foremost is the Association's ability to provide a forum for people with common interests to express their opinions and basic among these interests is the promotion of uniform feed regulations. Existence of this forum provides AAFCO members with a platform for deliberation and ultimately establishing policy.

When making decisions AAFCO acts as a deliberate body formulating policy through a series of discussions and votes thus eliminating rash decisions being made when emotions are high. A deliberating body cannot construct the best policy unless information is received from all quarters and therefore, the AAFCO forum allows for input from any interested party. Despite its deliberations AAFCO serves as one of the quickest ways of bringing about uniform policy change. Individual members can look to AAFCO for guidance when establishing their jurisdictional laws and regulations. The models and standards established by AAFCO have evolved over many years and continue to be modified in order to remain applicable. When establishing these models and standards it is incumbent upon AAFCO to make them equitable.

Standards of reference are also established whereby members and others can cite an official source for information on certain subjects such as ingredient definitions and official terms. When possible AAFCO also promotes the establishment of appropriate feed testing methodology. AAFCO also serves as the final decision maker when parties disagree on which way an AAFCO policy issue should be decided. This is crucial because without a final authority many AAFCO decisions would never be finalized. Decisions which are eventually finalized are arrived at using the democratic process.

AAFCO is also in a position to train regulatory of officials in the rigors of feed control. This is accomplished mainly through the annual Administration & Management of Feed Laws Seminar.

Since AAFCO plays such a large role in developing regulatory guidelines it is the duty of the organization to compile and disseminate this information. This is best handled through distribution of the annual official publication, which in many jurisdictions is truly official because of direct reference in a law.

Members of AAFCO are allowed an equal voice in the decision making process because any member from any jurisdictional delegation is allowed to be heard.

Larger delegations however, cannot over-whelm smaller delegations because of the one vote per jurisdiction rule. Since AAFCO cannot flourish without wide member participation it encourages administrative leaders to support their regulatory personnel in AAFCO activities through monetary as well as moral support. Inevitably once models and standards are established there will be differing interpretations of them. AAFCO has a vital role to play here also since it is the authority whose counsel can be sought to interpret the intent and spirit of the established models and standards. Enforcement of laws and regulations is most effective if administered uniformly and equitably. Often, enforcement involves more than one jurisdiction. AAFCO encourages and is sometimes indirectly involved in cooperative enforcement activities.

AAFCO PHILOSOPHY REGARDING FEED REGULATION

The most important aspect of feed regulation is to provide protection for the consumer as well as the regulated industry. Successful marketing of a product typically includes claims of content and performance. It could be argued that a product which does not live up to its claims would soon drop from the marketplace because it would not sustain repeat sales. However, subtle deviations from label claims may not be readily apparent and may result in health or production loses before use of the offending product can be discontinued. Therefore, a means of monitoring feed products to verify label claims needs to be established. Feed regulations can fulfill this need if they are established to include provisions for evaluating products for nutrient content, efficacy and safety.

Consumers are concerned about what they are purchasing and label disclosure can serve to inform them about product content. Armed with information about competing products the consumer can make an informed purchase decision. Feed regulations must be established which include the required, optional and prohibited label information. Unsubstantiated performance claims can be just as misleading to an unwary consumer as unsubstantiated nutrient claims, therefore a need exists for including prohibited label information in the regulations.

Labeling must also direct the consumer in proper use of the product. Directions may be as simple as naming the species for which the feed is intended or providing a lengthy explanation of the feeding rate. Feed regulations should include the minimum parameters which need to be met in order for a product to be considered adequate for its intended use. Feed regulations also serve to protect the feed industry from unfair competition and deceptive practices. Feed regulations need to be universally applied so each regulated party is required to follow the same rules. Any person who violates the rules must be brought into compliance or as a last resort eliminated from the marketplace. Feed regulations should also include a means by which those in violation of the regulations are known to the public including other industry members.

Feed regulations by themselves serve no useful purpose unless accompanied by a means of enforcement. Enforcement provisions must allow for the authority to verify compliance with the regulations. Punitive actions for noncompliance must be provided for in the regulations and need to be severe enough to act as a deterrent and yet not be crippling when imposed. Enforcement of regulations must be conducted by an independent and neutral group. Regulatory agencies must not have a vested interest in the outcome of enforcement and must not be accused of over zealous or complacent regulating. Wide surveillance of the industry, using the same investigatory and enforcement powers, will result in greater efficiency. Supporting isolated pockets of enforcement authority will tend to fragment the regulatory process and result in inefficient and costly programs. Ideally, feed regulations will become universal and uniform throughout the world. With the shrinking world economy through trade agreements and third world development this is no longer an unrealistic goal. A major function of feed regulation is to safeguard the health of man and animals. A list of substances acceptable as feed ingredients must be established including their designated names and definitions.

Standards should be set for substances determined to be unsafe in feed. When the unsafe substance is naturally occurring the standard could be incorporated in the feed ingredient definition by establishing a maximum allowable level. On site inspection authority should be made available to the feed control official to help assure production of safe products. Feed regulations must include the authority to conduct inspections and obtain samples for the purpose of detecting unsafe levels of substances, including the observation of conditions which may lead to feed contamination and the authority to require correction of these conditions if necessary. Products containing unsafe levels of substances or labeled in such a way as to be potentially unsafe should be kept from distribution. Such products may not only be harmful to the animals being fed but may also pose a contamination threat to the human food supply. Label requirements should be set which will help assure safe and effective use. Products determined to be nutritionally inadequate for their represented purpose should also be kept from the marketplace, thus helping safeguard animal health. Another important function of feed regulation is to provide a structure for orderly commerce. Feed regulation acts as a framework for simplifying and stabilizing a complex and diverse industry which in turn becomes an economic benefit to society by helping to establish an efficient system. In general feed regulations help prevent chaotic conditions in the marketplace.

Feed regulation is not without cost. The cost benefit ratio must be realistic and attainable. A tightly controlled feed industry may benefit society by guaranteeing the quality of each pound of feed sold, but the cost of such a program would be prohibitive. Conversely, a loosely controlled feed industry may be regulated with little cost but may result in unreliable or unsafe products. Determining the proper level of regulation between the two extremes is a most difficult task. In conclusion feed regulations should be developed which accomplish the basic goals of safeguarding the health of man and animals, establishing a structure for orderly commerce, and providing protection for consumers and the regulated industry. It is our hope that this document will serve as a reference for years to come in determining whether feed regulations are developed which reflect these basic goals. (Adopted 1990)

Part 2.
AAFCO Feeding Protocols for dog and cat foods

AAFCO FEEDING PROTOCOLS FOR
DOG AND CAT FOODS

MINIMUM FEEDING PROTOCOL FOR
PROVING AN UNQUALIFIED REPRESENTATION
OF NUTRITIONAL ADEQUACY FOR
A DOG OR CAT FOOD

The minimum testing necessary to prove nutritional adequacy may be obtained by using the gestation/lactation and the growth protocols. These protocols must be used sequentially. Thus, a manufacturer desiring to prove an unqualified claim for nutritional adequacy must use the litters obtained from performing the gestation/lactation protocol for the growth period. Test pups or kittens shall receive the test diet as their sole source of nourishment, other than dam's or queen's milk, during lactation and growth. Selection of pups or kittens shall be on a statistically sound basis from each of the litters qualifying for the gestation/lactation protocol with equal sex distribution preferred.

MINIMUM FEEDING PROTOCOL FOR PROVING AN ADULT MAINTENANCE CLAIM FOR A DOG FOOD

DOGS

A minimum of eight healthy adult dogs at least one year of age and of optimal body weight shall be required to start the test. Bitches in gestation or lactation shall be excluded. All animals starting the test must pass an initial physical examination by a veterinarian. A minimum of 30 dogs shall be required for developing a historical colony average, with data used to establish averages for all parameters coming from the same individual dogs. A minimum of eight dogs shall be required for the concurrent control group. Breed distribution shall be similar in all groups.

DIET

The same formulation shall be fed throughout the test although different production batches may be used. Diets fed to a concurrent control group or to dogs in the determination of historical colony averages must have successfully passed the minimum feeding protocol for an adult maintenance claim for a dog food. It may be helpful to consider diet type (i.e., dry vs. semimoist vs. canned) in establishing colony averages.

DURATION OF TEST

The test shall run for a minimum of 26 weeks and shall begin when dogs are placed on the test diet.

FEEDING PARAMETERS

The test diet shall be the sole source of nutrients except for water. Dogs shall be fed ad libitum or based on energy needs. Fresh water shall be provided ad libitum. Any interruption in feeding protocol must be disclosed and may invalidate the test.

CLINICAL OBSERVATIONS AND MEASUREMENTS

1. Daily food consumption may be measured and recorded.

2. Individual body weights shall be measured and recorded at the beginning, weekly, and at the end of the test.

OPTIONAL PROCEDURES

The testing requirements for a maintenance dog food may be met by successfully performing either the growth or gestation/lactation protocols in lieu of performing the maintenance protocol.

MINIMUM FEEDING PROTOCOL FOR PROVING AN ADULT MAINTENANCE CLAIM FOR A CAT FOOD

CATS

A minimum of eight healthy adult cats at least one year of age and of optimal body weight shall be required to start the test. Queens in gestation or lactation shall be excluded. All animals starting the test must pass an initial physical examination by a veterinarian. A minimum of 30 cats shall be required for developing a historical colony average, with data used to establish averages for all parameters coming from the same individual cats. A minimum of eight cats shall be required for the concurrent control group.

DIET

The same formulation shall be fed throughout the test although different production batches may be used. Diets fed to a concurrent control group or to cats in the determination of historical colony averages must have successfully passed a minimum feeding protocol for an adult maintenance claim for a cat food. It may be helpful to consider diet type (i.e., dry vs. semimoist vs. canned) in establishing colony averages.

DURATION OF TEST

The test shall run for a minimum of 26

weeks and shall begin when cats are placed on the test diet.

FEEDING PARAMETERS
The test diet shall be the sole source of nutrients except for water. Cats shall be fed ad libitum or based on energy needs. Fresh water shall be provided ad libitum. Any interruption in feeding protocol must be disclosed and may invalidate the test.

CLINICAL OBSERVATIONS
AND MEASUREMENTS
1. Daily food consumption may be measured and recorded.
2. Individual body weights shall be measured and recorded at the beginning, weekly, and at the end of the test.
3. Hemoglobin, packed cell volume, serum alkaline phosphatase, serum albumin and whole blood taurine shall be measured and recorded at the end of the test.
4. All cats shall be given a complete physical examination by a veterinarian at the beginning and at the end of the test. Each cat shall be evaluated as to general health, body and hair coat condition, and comments shall be recorded.
5. Any medication and the reason for its use must be recorded.
6. A number of cats, not to exceed 25% of those starting the test, may be removed for non-nutritional reasons or poor food intake. The

reason for their removal must be recorded. Cats may be removed for poor food intake only during the first two weeks of the test. Data already collected from cats weaned. All puppies starting the test must pass an initial physical examination by a veterinarian. An equal sex distribution is recommended for all groups. If equal sex distribution is not feasible, appropriate corrections must be made. A minimum of 30 puppies shall be required for developing the historical colony average, with data used to establish averages for all parameters coming from the same individual puppies. A minimum of eight puppies from three different bitches (same sex distribution as the test group) shall be required for the concurrent control group. Breed distribution shall be similar in all groups.

DIET
The same formulation shall be fed throughout the test, although different production batches may be used. Diets fed to a concurrent control group or to puppies in the determination of historical colony averages must have successfully passed a minimum feeding protocol for a growth claim for a dog food. It may be helpful to consider diet type (i.e., dry vs. semimoist vs. canned) in establishing colony averages.

DURATION OF TEST
The test shall run for a minimum of 10 weeks.

FEEDING PARAMETERS

The test diet shall be the sole source of nutrients except for water. Puppies shall be fed ad libitum or based on energy needs. Fresh water shall be provided ad libitum. Puppies may be fed individually or in groups. The historical or concurrent control groups shall be fed in a manner similar to that of the treatment group. Any interruption in feeding protocol must be disclosed and may invalidate the test.

CLINICAL OBSERVATIONS AND MEASUREMENTS

1. Daily food consumption may be measured and recorded.

2. Individual body weights shall be measured and recorded at the beginning, weekly, and at the end of the test.

3. Hemoglobin, packed cell volume, and serum albumin shall be measured and recorded at the end of the test.

4. All puppies shall be given a complete physical examination by a veterinarian at the beginning and at the end of the test. Each puppy shall be evaluated as to general health, body and hair coat condition, and comments shall be recorded.

5. Any medication and the reason for its use must be recorded.

6. A number of puppies, not to exceed 25% of those starting the test, may be removed for non-nutritional reasons or poor food intake.

The reason for their removal must be recorded. Puppies may be removed for poor food intake only during the first two weeks of the test. Data already collected from puppies removed from the test shall be retained although it does not have to be included in the final results.

7. A necropsy shall be conducted on any puppy which dies during the test and the findings recorded.

INTERPRETATION

A. The diet shall fail if any puppy shows clinical or pathological signs of nutritional deficiency or excess.

B. All puppies not removed for non-nutritional reasons or poor food intake must successfully finish the test.

C. The average body weight gain shall not be less than either:

1. 75% of the historical colony average, with averages for males and females determined separately for both the test and colony groups- or

2. The historical colony average minus 2.33 times the standard error. The standard error is defined as the colony standard deviation divided by the square root of the number of test animals- or

3. The average for the concurrent control group, minus the allowance for normal variation. The allowance for normal variation is defined as 2.62 times the pooled estimate of the standard error of the difference of the two group averages

(one-tailed, two sample t-test at p <0.01, if n =8 per group).

D. The average final hemoglobin, packed cell volume and serum albumin values shall not be less than either:

1. Hemoglobin - 11.0 g/dl (no individual < 9.0 g/dl) PCV - 33% (no individual <27%) Albumin - 2.6 g/dl (no individual < 2.2 g/dl); or

2. The historical colony average minus 2.33 times the standard error. The standard error is defined as the colony standard deviation divided by the square root of the number of test animals; or

3. The average for the concurrent control group, minus the allowance for normal variation. The allowance for normal variation is defined as 2.62 times the pooled estimate of the standard error of the difference of the two group averages (one-tailed, two sample t-test at p <0.01, if n =8 per group).

MINIMUM FEEDING PROTOCOL FOR PROVING A GROWTH CLAIM FOR A CAT FOOD

KITTENS

A minimum of eight kittens from three different queens shall be required to start the test. The kittens shall be no older than nine weeks of age and weaned. All kittens starting the test must pass an initial physical examination by a veterinarian. An equal sex distribution is recommended for all groups. If equal sex distribution is not feasible, appropriate corrections must be made. A minimum of 30 kittens shall be required for developing the historical colony average, with data used to establish averages for all parameters coming from the same individual kittens. A minimum of eight kittens from three different queens (same sex distribution as the test group) shall be required for the concurrent control group.

DIET
The same formulation shall be fed throughout the test, although different production batches may be used. Diets fed to a concurrent control group or to kittens in the determination of historical colony averages must have successfully passed a minimum feeding protocol for a growth claim for a cat food. It may be helpful to consider diet type (i.e., dry vs. semimoist vs. canned) in establishing colony averages.

DURATION OF TEST
The test shall run for a minimum of 10 weeks.

FEEDING PARAMETERS
The test diet shall be the sole source of nutrients except for water. Kittens shall be fed ad libitum or according to energy needs. Fresh water shall be provided ad libitum. Kittens may be fed individually or in groups. Historical or concurrent control groups shall be fed in a man-

ner similar to that of the treatment group. Any interruption in feeding protocol must be disclosed and may invalidate the test.

CLINICAL OBSERVATIONS
AND MEASUREMENTS

1. Daily food consumption may be measured and recorded.

2. Individual body weights shall be measured and recorded at the beginning, weekly, and at the end of the test.

3. Hemoglobin, packed cell volume, whole blood taurine, and serum albumin shall be measured and recorded at the end of the test.

4. All kittens shall be given a complete physical examination by a veterinarian at the beginning and at the end of the test. Each kitten shall be evaluated as to general health, body and hair coat condition, and comments shall be recorded.

5. Any medication and the reason for its use must be recorded.

6. A number of kittens, not to exceed 25% of those starting the test, may be removed for non-nutritional reasons or poor food intake. The reason for their removal must be recorded. Kittens may be removed for poor food intake only during the first two weeks of the test. Data already collected from kittens removed from the test shall be retained although it does not have to be included in the final results.

7. A necropsy shall be conducted on any

kitten which dies during the test and the findings recorded.

INTERPRETATION

A. The diet shall fail if any kitten shows clinical or pathological signs of nutritional deficiency or excess.

B. All kittens not removed for non-nutritional reasons or poor food intake must successfully finish the test.

C. The average body weight gain shall not be less than either:

1. 80% of the historical colony average, with averages for males and females determined separately for both the test and colony groups; or

2. The historical colony average minus 2.33 times the standard error. The standard error is defined as the colony standard deviation divided by the square root of the number of test animals; or

3. The average for the concurrent control group, minus the allowance for normal variation. The allowance for normal variation is defined as 2.62 times the pooled estimate of the standard error of the difference of the two group averages (one- tailed, two sample t-test at p-.0l, if n=8 per group).

D. The average final hemoglobin, packed cell volume, whole blood taurine and serum albumin values shall not be less than either:

1. Hemoglobin - 10.0 g/dl (no individual < 8.0 g/dl) PCV - 29% (no individual < 26%) Taurine

- 300 nmole/ml (no individual <200 nmole/ ml)
Albumin - 2.7 g/dl (no individual < 2.4 g/dl); or

2. The historical colony average minus 2.33 times the standard error. The standard error is defined as the colony standard deviation divided by the square root of the number of test animals; or

3. The average for the concurrent control group, minus the allowance for normal variation. The allowance for normal variation is defined as 2.62 times the pooled estimate of the standard error of the difference of the two group averages (one-tailed, two sample t-test at p-O.01, if n=8 per group).

MINIMUM FEEDING PROTOCOL FOR PROVING A GESTATION/LACTATION CLAIM FOR A DOG FOOD

DOGS

Enough bitches shall be used to ensure that a minimum of eight pregnant bitches start the test. The bitches must be in at least their second heat period and at least one year of age. All bitches starting the test must pass an initial physical examination by a veterinarian. There is no specific size or breed requirement, but the bitches and studs must be of the same breed. A minimum of 30 bitches shall be required for developing a historical colony average, with data used to establish averages for all parameters coming from the same individual bitches. A minimum of eight bitches shall be required for the concurrent control group. Breed distribution must be similar in all groups. For larger litters, puppies may be removed to normalize litter size to the following levels: Adult Dog Weights Number in Litter Less than 20# 5 20-50# 6 Greater than 50# 8   Removed puppies may be transferred to bitches of the same breed with smaller litters.

DIET

The same formulation shall be fed throughout the test, although different production batches may be used. Diets fed to a concurrent control group or to bitches in the determination of historical colony averages must have successfully passed the minimum feeding protocol for a gestation/lactation claim for a dog food. It may be helpful to consider diet type (i.e., dry vs. semimoist vs. canned) in establishing colony averages.

DURATION OF TEST

The test shall begin at or before estrus, and shall end when the puppies are 4 weeks of age, independent of age at weaning.

FEEDING PARAMETERS

The test diet shall be the sole source of nutrients except for water. Animals shall be fed ad libitum or based on energy needs. Fresh water shall be provided ad libitum. Any interruption in feeding protocol must be disclosed, and may invalidate the test.

CLINICAL OBSERVATIONS
AND MEASUREMENTS

1. Daily food consumption for the bitch during gestation and for the bitch and her puppies during lactation may be measured and recorded.

2. For each bitch, body weights shall be measured and recorded at breeding, weekly during gestation, within 24 hours after whelping, weekly during lactation, and at the end of the test. For the puppies, body weights shall be measured and recorded within 24 hours after birth, weekly, and at the end of test.

3. The litter size at birth, at one day of age, and at the end of the test shall be recorded. Stillbirths and congenital abnormalities shall be recorded.

4. Hemoglobin, packed cell volume, and serum albumin shall be measured and recorded for the bitch at the end of the test.

5. All bitches shall be given a complete physical examination by a veterinarian at the beginning of the test, and at the end of the test. Each bitch shall be evaluated as to general health, body and hair coat condition, and comments shall be recorded. All puppies shall be given a complete physical examination by a veterinarian within 72 hours after birth, and at the end of the test. Each puppy shall be evaluated as to general

health, body and hair coat condition, and comments shall be recorded.

6. Any medication and the reason for its use must be recorded.

7. A number of bitches, not to exceed 25% of those starting the test, may be removed for non-nutritional reasons or poor food intake. The reason for their removal must be recorded. Bitches may be removed for poor food intake only during the first two weeks of the test. Data already collected from bitches or puppies removed from the test shall be retained although it does not have to be included in the final results.

8. A necropsy shall be conducted on any bitch or puppy which dies during the test and the findings recorded.

INTERPRETATION

A. The diet shall fail if any bitch or puppy shows clinical or pathological signs of nutritional deficiency or excess.

B. All bitches not removed for non-nutritional reasons or poor food intake must successfully finish the test. Eighty percent of all one-day-old puppies must survive and successfully finish the test.

C. The pregnant bitches on the test shall show weight gain during gestation. The average percent body weight change (breeding through the end of the test) of the bitches shall not be less than either:

1. The historical colony average minus

2.33 times the standard error. The standard error is defined as the colony standard deviation divided by the square root of the number of test animals; or

2. The average for the concurrent control group, minus the allowance for normal variation. The allowance for normal variation is defined as 2.62 times the pooled estimate of the standard error of the difference of the two group averages (one-tailed, two sample t-test at p<0.01, if n=8 per group).

D. The average weight of the puppies at the end of the test shall not be less than either:
1. 75% of the historical colony average; or
2. The historical colony average minus 2.33 times the standard error. The standard error is defined as the colony standard deviation divided by the square root number of test animals- or

3. The average for the concurrent control group, minus the allowance for normal variation. The allowance for normal variation is defined as 2.62 times the pooled estimate of the standard error of the difference of the two group averages (one-tailed, two sample t-test at p&0.01, if n=8 per group).

E. At the end of the test, the average litter size of the bitches completing the test shall not be less than either:
1. 80% of the historical colony average; or
2. The historical colony average minus 2.33 times the standard error. The standard error is defined as the colony standard deviation di-

vided by the square root number of test animals; or

3. The average for the concurrent control group, minus the allowance for normal variation. The allowance for normal variation is defined as 2.62 times the pooled estimate of the standard error of the difference of the two group averages (one- tailed, two sample t-test at p50.01, if n=8 per group).

F. The average final hemoglobin, packed cell volume, and serum albumin values shall not be less than either:

1. Hemoglobin - 10.0 g/dl (no individual <8.0 g/dl) PCV - 30% (no individual < 24%) Albumin - 2.4 g/dl (no individual < 2.2 g/dl); or

2. The historical colony average minus 2.33 times the standard error. The standard error is defined as the colony standard deviation divided by the square root of the number of test animals; or

3. The average for the concurrent control group, minus the allowance for normal variation. The allowance for normal variation is defined as 2.62 times the pooled estimate of the standard error of the difference of the two group averages (one-tailed, two sample t-test at p-0.01, if n=8 per group).

MINIMUM FEEDING PROTOCOL FOR PROVING A GESTATION/LACTATION CLAIM FOR A CAT FOOD

CATS

Enough queens shall be used to ensure that a minimum of eight pregnant queens start the test. The queens must be in at least their second heat period and at least one year of age. All queens starting the test must pass an initial physical examination by a veterinarian. A minimum of 30 queens shall be required for developing a historical colony average, with data used to establish averages for all parameters coming from the same individual queens. A minimum of eight queens shall be required for the concurrent control group. For litters larger than 5 kittens, the additional kittens may be removed. Removed kittens may be transferred to queens with smaller litters.

DIET

The same formulation shall be fed throughout the test, although different production batches may be used. Diets fed to a concurrent control group or to queens in the determination of historical colony averages must have successfully passed the minimum feeding protocol for a gestation/lactation claim for a cat food. It may be helpful to consider diet type (i.e., dry vs. semimoist vs. canned) in establishing colony averages.

DURATION OF TEST

The test shall begin at or before estrus, and shall end when the kittens are 6 weeks of age, independent of age at weaning.

FEEDING PARAMETERS

The test diet shall be the sole source of nutrients except for water. Animals shall be fed ad libitum or based on energy needs. Fresh water shall be provided ad libitum. Any interruption in feeding protocol must be disclosed, and may invalidate the test.

CLINICAL OBSERVATIONS AND MEASUREMENTS

1. Daily food consumption for the queen during gestation and for the queen and her kittens during lactation may be measured and recorded.

2. For each queen, body weights shall be measured and recorded at breeding, weekly during gestation, within 24 hours after queening, weekly during lactation, and at the end of the test. For the kittens, body weights shall be measured and recorded within 24 hours after birth, weekly, and at the end of the test.

3. The litter size at birth, at one day of age, and at the end of the test shall be recorded. Stillbirths and congenital abnormalities shall be recorded.

4. Hemoglobin, packed cell volume, whole blood taurine, and serum albumin shall be mea-

sured for the queen at the end of the test.

5. All queens shall be given a complete physical examination by a veterinarian at the beginning of the test and at the end of the test. Each queen shall be evaluated as to general health, body and hair coat condition, and comments shall be recorded. All kittens shall be given a complete physical examination by a veterinarian within 72 hours after birth, and at the end of the test. Each kitten shall be evaluated as to general health, body and hair coat condition, and comments shall be recorded.

6. Any medication and the reason for its use must be recorded.

7. A number of queens, not to exceed 25% of those starting the test, may be removed for non-nutritional reasons or poor food intake. The reason for their removal must be recorded. Queens may be removed for poor food intake only during the first two weeks of the test. Data already collected from queens or kittens removed from the test shall be retained although it does not have to be included in the final results.

8. A necropsy shall be conducted on any queen or kitten which dies during the test and findings recorded.

INTERPRETATION

A. The diet shall fail if any queen or kitten shows clinical or pathological signs of nutritional deficiency or excess.

B. All queens not removed for non-nutritional

reasons or poor food intake must successfully finish the test. Eighty percent of all one-day-old kittens must survive and successfully finish the test.

C. The pregnant queens on the test shall show weight gain during gestation. The average percent body weight change (breeding through the end of the test) of the queens shall not be less than either:

    1. Negative ten percent (no individual <-15%); or

    2. The historical colony average minus 2.33 times the standard error. The standard error is defined as the colony standard deviation divided by the square root of the number of test animals: or

    3. The average for the concurrent control group, minus the allowance for normal variation. The allowance for normal variation is defined as 2.62 times the pooled estimate of the standard error of the difference of the two group averages (one-tailed, two sample t-test at p<0.01, if n=8 per group).

D. The average weight of the kittens at the end of the test shall not be less than either:

    1. 80% of the historical colony average; or

    2. The historical colony average minus 2.33 times the standard error. The standard error is defined as the colony standard deviation divided by the square root number of test animals; or

    3. The average for the concurrent control

group, minus the allowance for normal variation. The allowance for normal variation is defined as 2.62 times the pooled estimate of the standard error of the difference of the two group averages (one-tailed, two sample t-test at p <0.01, if n=8 per group).

E. At the end of the test, the average litter size of the queens completing the test shall not be less than either:

1. 80% of the historical colony average; or

2. The historical colony average minus 2.33 times the standard error. The standard error is defined as the colony standard deviation divided by the square root number of test animals; or

3. The average for the concurrent control group, minus the allowance for normal variation. The allowance for normal variation is defined as 2.62 times the pooled estimate of the standard error of the difference of the two group averages (one-tailed, two sample t-test at p-0.01, if n=8 per group).

F. The average final hemoglobin, packed cell volume, whole blood taurine and serum albumin values shall not be less than either:

1. Hemoglobin - 9.5 g/dl (no individual < 8.0 g/dl) PCV - 29% (no individual < 26%) Taurine - 300 nmole/ml (no individual < 200 nmole/ ml) Albumin - 2.7 g/dl (no individual < 2.4 g/dl); or

2. The historical colony average minus 2.33 times the standard error. The standard error is defined as the colony standard deviation di-

vided by the square root of the number of test animals, or

3. The average for the concurrent control group, minus the allowance for normal variation. The allowance for normal variation is defined as 2.62 times the pooled estimate of the standard error of the difference of the two group averages (one-tailed, two sample t-test at p-0.01, if n=8 per group).

NUTRIENT PROFILES FOR DOG FOODS
TABLE 1 AAFCO NUTRIENT
PROFILES FOR DOG FOODS

Nutrient	Units DM Basis	Growth & Repro Min	Adult Maint Min	Max
Protein	%	22.0	18.0	
Arginine	%	0.62	0.51	
Histidine	%	0.22	0.18	
Isoleucine	%	0.45	0-37	
Leucine	%	0.72	0.59	
Lysine	%	0.77	0.63	
Methionine-cystine		0.53	0.43	
Phenylalanine-tyrosine		0.89	0.73	
Threonine	%	0.58	0.48	
Tryptophan	%	0.20	0.16	
Valine	%	0.48	0.39	
Fat	%	8.0	5.0	
Linoleic acid	%	1.0	1.0	
Minerals				
Calcium	%	1.0	0.6	2.5
Phosphorus	%	0.8	0.5	1.6
Ca:P ratio	%	1:1	1:1	2:1
Potassium	%	0.6	0.6	
Sodium	%	0.3	0.06	
Chloride	%	0.45	0.09	
Magnesium	%	0.04	0.04	0.3
Iron	mg/kg	80	80	3000
Copper	mg/kg	7.3	7.3	250
Manganese	mg/kg	5.0	5.0	
Zinc	mg/kg	120	120	1000
Iodine	mg/kg	1.5	1.5	50
Selenium	mg/kg	0.11	0.11	2
Vitamins				
Vitamin A	IU/kg	5000	5000	250000
Vitamin D	IU/kg	500	500	5000
Vitamin E	IU/kg	50	50	1000
Thiamine	mg/kg	1.0	1.0	
Riboflavin	mg/kg	2.2	2.2	
Pantothenic Acid	mg/kg	10	10	
Niacin	mg/kg	11.4	11.4	
Pyridoxine	mg/kg	1.0	1.0	
Folic Acid	mg/kg	0.18	0.18	
Vitamin B12	mg/kg	0.022	0.022	
Choline	mg/kg	1200	1200	

PRESUMES an energy density of 3.5 kcal ME/g DM.
Rations greater than 4.0 kcal/g should be corrected for energy density. Dog Food Nutrient Profiles
131

TABLE 2
AAFCO NUTRIENT PROFILES FOR
DOG FOODS BASED ON CALORIC DENSITY

Nutrient	Units per 1000 kcal ME	Growth & Repro Min	Adult Maint Min	Max
Protein	g	62.9	51.4	
Arginine	g	1.77	1.46	
Histidine	g	0.63	0.51	
Isoleucine	g	1.29	1.06	
Leucine	g	2.06	1.69	
Lysine	g	2.20	1.80	
Methionine-cystine	g	1.51	1.23	
Phenylalanine-tyrosine	g	2.54	2.09	
Threonine	g	1.66	1.37	
Tryptophan	g	0.57	0.46	
Valine	g	1.37	1.11	
Fat	g	22.9	14.3	
Linoleic acid	g	2.9	2.9	
Minerals				
Calcium	g	2.9	1.7	7.1
Phosphorus	g	2.3	1.4	4.6
Potassium	g	1.7	1.7	
Sodium	g	0.86	0.17	
Chloride	g	1.29	0.26	
Magnesium	g	0.11	0.11	0.86
Iron	mg	23	23	857
Copper	mg	2.1	2.1	71
Manganese	mg	1.4	1.4	
Zinc	mg	34	34	286
Iodine	mg	0.43	0.43	14
Selenium	mg	0.03	0.03	0.57
Vitamins Vitamin A	IU	1429	1429	71429
Vitamin D	IU	143	143	1429
Vitamin E	IU	14	14	286
Thiamine	mg	0.29	0.29	
Riboflavin	mg	0.63	0.63	
Pantothenic Acid	mg	2.9	2.9	
Niacin	mg	3.3	3.3	
Pyridoxine	mg	0.29	0.29	
Folic Acid	mg	0.05	0.05	
Vitamin B12	mg	0.006	0.006	
Choline	mg	343	343	

TABLE 3
Examples of correction of the minimum levels for growth and reproduction for varying moisture and caloric density

	Moisture Kcal/g DM	DM Basis 0 3.5	Dry Food 10 3.5	Canned 75 4.3 Nutrient
Units				
Protein	%	22.0	19.8	6.8
Arginine	%	0.62	0.56	0.19
Histidine	%	0.22	0.20	0.07
Isoleucine	%	0.45	0.41	0.14
Leucine	%	0.72	0.65	0.22
Lysine	%	0.77	0.69	0.24
Methionine-cystin	%	0.53	0.48	0.16
Phenylalanine-tyrosine		0.89	0.80	0.27
Threonine	%	0.58	0.52	0.18
Tryptophan	%	0.20	0.18	0.06
Valine	%	0.48	0.43	0.15
Fat	%	8.0	7.2	2.5
Linoleic acid	%	1.0	0.9	0.3
Minerals				

Calcium	%	1.0	0.9	0.3
Phosphorus	%	0.8	0.72	0.25
Potassium	%	0.6	0.54	0.18
Sodium	%	0.3	0.27	0.09
Chloride	%	0.45	0.41	0.14
Magnesium	%	0.04	0.04	0.012
Iron	mg/kg	80	72	25
Copper	mg/kg	7.3	6.6	2.2
Manganese	mg/kg	5.0	4.5	1.5
Zinc	mg/kg	120	108	37
Iodine	mg/kg	1.5	1.35	0.46
Selenium	mg/kg	0.11	0.10	0.03
Vitamins & others				
Vitamin A	IU/kg	5000	4500	1536
Vitamin D	IU/kg	500	450	154
Vitamin E	IU/kg	50	45	15
Thiamine	mg/kg	1.0	0.9	0.3
Riboflavin	mg/kg	2.2	2.0	0.7
Pantothenic Acid	mg/kg	10	9	3
Niacin	mg/kg	11.4	10.3	3.5
Pyridoxine	mg/kg	1.0	0.9	0.3
Folic Acid	mg/kg	0.18	0.16	0.06
Vitamin B12	mg/kg	0.022	0.020	0.007
Choline	mg/kg	1200	1080	369

Table 1 represents the nutrient levels for dog foods upon which values
for the subsequent tables were based. Levels in Table 1 are given on a dry
matter basis at a defined energy density of 3.5 kcal ME/g DM.
Table 2 offers the same information, but in terms of energy density. Table
3 demonstrates two examples of correcting the levels to account for
variances in moisture or energy density.

CORRECTING FOR
DRY MATTER/MOISTURE CONTENT

The values as given in Table 1 are listed in terms
of dry matter (DM). However, the values listed in
the guaranteed analysis on dog food labels or
reported from laboratories are most often given
on an "as is" or "as fed" (AF) basis. The difference between a value reported on a DM basis vs
an AF basis is inversely proportional to the moisture (water) content of the food. The higher the
moisture content, the lower the AF value would
be compared to its DM value. This discrepancy
makes direct comparison between the food and
the table values impossible without first correcting one or the other sets of values so that both

are on an equal dry matter basis.

One method of correcting for moisture is the adjustment of the values listed in the guaranteed analysis or reported from a laboratory on an AF basis to a DM basis before a comparison with the table values is made. This is done by dividing each AF value by the proportion of DM in the food [(100 % moisture)/ 100].

Example A: A dry dog food making a growth claim bears the following guaranteed analysis:

	Guarantee	Table 1 Minimum Level	Moisture adjusted guarantee	Adjusted guarantee vs Table 1
Crude Protein:	min. 21%	22%	23.3%	OK
Crude fat:	min. 8%	8%	8.9%	OK
Crude fiber:	max. 4%			
Moisture:	max. 10%	0%	0%	
Ash:	max. 8%			
Calcium:	min. 0.9%	1.0%	1.0%	OK
Phosphorus:	min. 0.75%	0.8%	0.83%	OK

Directly comparing the values in Example A for protein, calcium, and phosphorus as stated in the guarantee to the minimum values for growth given in Table 1, this food would appear to be deficient. However, this comparison is not valid, since the values for the food are listed on a 10 Ss moisture (90% DM) basis, while the table values are given on a 0% moisture (100% DM) basis. To put both sets of values on an equal moisture basis, the guaranteed values were adjusted to 100% DM by dividing each value by the proportion DM of the food in question (0.9%) With this correction, it becomes apparent that the moisture adjusted guaranteed percentages of the reported nutrients do, in fact, meet the minimum levels for growth.

As an alternative method to converting the guaranteed values to a DM basis, the table values can be adjusted to match the moisture content of the food in question. This can be achieved by simply multiplying each table value by the proportion DM of the food (in this example, 0.9%). Such a calculation yields the following:

	Guarantee	Table 1 Minimum Level	Moisture adjusted table value	Guarantee vs adjusted Table 1
Crude Protein:	min. 21%	22%	19.8%	OK
Crude fat:	min. 8%	8%	7.2%	OK
Crude fiber:	max. 4%			
Moisture:	max. 10%	0%	10%	
Ash:	max. 8%			
Calcium:	min. 0.9%	1.0%	0.9%	OK
Phosphorus:	min. 0.75%	0.8%	0.72%	OK

Again, with correction, the guaranteed percentages meet the moisture adjusted minimum levels for growth. A more complete example of correction of the table values to a 10% moisture (90% DM) basis is found in the second column of Table 3.

CORRECTING FOR ENERGY DENSITY

The values given in Table 1 presume an energy density of 3.5 kilocalories of metabolizable energy per gram of food on a dry matter basis (3.5 kcal ME/g DM). Many dog foods will have energy densities close to this amount, and correction is not necessary. However, canned or other high-fat foods may have DM energy densities considerably higher than the presumed value. When these higher energy-dense products are fed, the dog will require less of the food to meet its caloric requirements. Under these circumstances, the concentrations of the other nutrients in the food would have to be increased proportionately, so that the dog would receive the needed amount of each nutrient in the smaller amount of food. Therefore, when the estimated energy density of the food exceeds 4.0 kcal ME/g DM, the nutrient levels should be corrected for caloric content before valid comparisons can be made.

Conversely, a low-fat/high-fiber product could be much lower than 3.5 kcaUg in energy density. Theoretically, a lower concentration of the other nutrients should be required, assuming that the dog is allowed and able to consume enough of the product to meet its caloric needs. Since this assumption does not always hold true, however, low-energy rations should not be corrected for energy density. Furthermore, a low-energy density product should not be considered as adequate for growth and reproductive needs, regardless of the levels of the other nutrients.

The first step is the determination of the energy density of the food in question. When this value is not known by actual digestibility trial data, the metabolizable energy content of a food can be estimated from the values derived from a proximate or guaranteed analysis by use of the following equation:

ME (kcaUg) = [(3.5 X P) + (8.5 X F) + (3.5 X C)]/100 where P = % crude protein, F = %

crude fat, and C = % carbohydrates (nitrogen-free extract). Percent carbohydrates is defined as 100% less the total of percentages for crude protein, crude fat, crude fiber, moisture, and ash. This calculation for ME is on an AF basis. To determine ME on a DM basis, the value should be divided by the proportion DM as determined from the analysis [(100 % moisture)/100].

Following the determination of the energy density of the food in question, the nutrient values can be converted to an energy basis equal to those in Table 1.

Example B: A canned-type food making a growth claim bears the following guaranteed analysis:

	Guarantee	Table 1 Minimum Level	Moisture adjusted guarantee	Energy adjusted guarantee	E-adjusted guarantee vs Table 1	
Crude protein:	min. 8%	22%	32%	26%		OK
Crude fat:	min. 6%	8%	24%	19.5%		OK
Crude fiber:	max. 1%					
Moisture:	max. 75%		0%	0%		
Ash:	max. 2%					
Calcium:	min. 0.25%	1.0%	1.0%	0.8%		LOW
Phosphorus:	min. 0.2%	0.8%	0.8%	0.65%		LOW
Energy:	1.07AF	3.5 DM	4.3 DM	3.5 DM		

A cursory examination of the values listed in the guaranteed analysis compared to the minimum values given in Table 1 revealed that a direct comparison would not be valid. Since the food in question was 75% moisture (25% DM), the major reason for the discrepancy was likely due to water content. By first dividing the guaranteed values by the proportion DM (0.25), the moisture-adjusted guaranteed values were derived. Comparing these corrected values with the table values, this food appeared to meet the minimums for a growth claim.

However, in this example, direct comparison of the moisture-adjusted guaranteed values with the table values was premature. The high DM fat content of the food in question compared to the standard (24% vs 8%) was an indication that the food was probably more energy-dense than the table value of 3.5 kcaUg DM. When calculated, in fact, it was found to be 4.3 kcaUg DM (1.07 kcaUg AF). Therefore a second adjustment to account for the differences in energy density was warranted. This was achieved by dividing each moisture-adjusted guaranteed value by 4.3 (the DM energy density of the food) and then multiplying the result by 3.5 (the standard energy density). This second manipulation revealed that the energy-adjusted guarantees for calcium and phosphorus were, in fact, below minimum levels for growth.

In this example, the guaranteed values were corrected for moisture first, then energy. However, a direct correction for energy could also have been done without regard for moisture content. Dividing the AF values in the guaranteed analysis by the AF energy density (1.07 kcaUg),and then multiplying the result by 3.5 would have yielded values similar to those listed in the last column above. As demonstrated with moisture-correction methods above, an alternative to correcting the values of the food to meet the table energy density is correcting the table values to meet the food's energy density. Below, each table value was divided by 3.5, and the result was multiplied by the appropriate energy density value (1.07). If we had first corrected the table values for moisture, the appropriate multiplier would have been 4.3.

	Guarantee	Table 1 Minimum level	Energy adjusted table value	Guarantee vs adjusted Table 1
Crude protein:	min. 8%	22%	6.8%	OK
Crude fat:	min. 6%	8%	2.5%	OK
Crude fiber:	max. 1%			
Moisture:	max. 75%			
Ash:	max. 2%			
Calcium	min. 0.25%	1.0%	0.3%	LOW
Phosphorus:	min. 0.2%	0.8%	0.25%	LOW
Energy:		1.07 AF	3.5 DM	1.07 AF

Note that although the energy-adjusted minimum for fat calculated out to be 2.5%, a much higher level of fat (in this case, 6%) predefined the higher energy density and dictated the need for energy adjustment in the first place. Since a higher level of fat, for the most part, predetermines what the higher energy density will be, the energy-adjusted table minimum value for fat should always be met and will often be grossly exceeded. A more complete example of correction of the table values to a 4.3 kcal ME/g DM basis is found in the last column of Table 3.

The last method of correcting for energy density is to convert the values given for the food to an energy ("per 1000 kcal") basis, and to then compare these values with those listed in Table 2 instead of Table 1.

	Guarantee	Table 2 Minimum amount	Energy based "per 1000 kcal" guarantee	Energy based guarantee vs Table 2
Crude protein:	min. 8%	62.9 g	74.8 g	OK
Crude fat:	min. 6%	22.9 g	56.1 g	OK
Crude fiber:	max. 1%			
Moisture:	max. 75%			
Ash:	max. 2%			

Calcium:	min. 0.25%	2.9 g	2.3 g	LOW
Phosphorus:	min 0.2%	2.3 g	1.9 g	LOW

To convert percentages to grams per 1000 kilocalories (g/1000 kcal), the percent value was divided by the energy density (in this example, 1.07 kcaVg), and then the result multiplied by 10. If we had wished to convert milligrams or International Units per kilogram (mg/kg or lU/kg) to mg or IU per 1000 kcal, then the value would just be divided by the energy density in kcaUg.

The rationale for development of the nutrient profiles for dog foods can be found in the 1992 Official Publication starting on page 288

NUTRIENT PROFILES FOR CAT FOODS
TABLE 1 AAFCO Nutrient Profiles for Cat Foods

Nutrient	Units DM Basis	Growth & Repro Min	Adult Maint Min	Max
Protein	%	30.0	26.0	
Arginine	%	1.25	1.04	
Histidine	%	0.31	0.31	
Isoleucine	%	0.52	0.52	
Leucine	%	1.25	1.25	
Lysine	%	1.20	0.83	
Methionine-cystine	%	1.10	1.10	
Methionine	%	0.62	0.62	1.5
Phenylalanine-tyrosine	%	0.88	0.88	
Phenylalanine	%	0.42	0.42	
Taurine (extruded)	%	0.10	0.10	
Taurine (canned)	%	0.20	0.20	
Threonine	%	0.73	0-73	
Tryptophan	%	0.25	0.16	
Valine	%	0.62	0.62	
Fatb	%	9.0	9.0	
Linoleic acid	%	0.5	0.5	
Arachidonic acid	%	0.02	0.02	
Minerals				
Calcium	%	1.0	0.6	
Phosphorus	%	0.8	0.5	
Potassium	%	0.6	0.6	
Sodium	%	0.2	0.2	
Chloride	%	03	03	
MagnesiumC	%	0.08	0.04	
Iron d	mg/kg	80	80	
Copper	mg/kg	5	5	
Iodine	mg/kg	0.35	0.35	
Zinc	mg/kg	75	75	2000
Manganese	mg/kg	7.5	7.5	
Selenium	mg/kg	0.1	0.1	
Vitamins				
Vitamin A	IU/kg	9000	5000	750000
Vitamin D	lU/kg	750	500	10000

Vitamin Ee	IU/kg	30	30
Vitamin Kf	mg/kg	0.1	0.1
Thiamineg	mg/kg	5.0	5.0
Riboflavin	mg/kg	4.0	4.0
Pyridoxine	mg/kg	4.0	4.0
Niacin	mg/kg	60	60
Pantothenic Acid	mg/kg	5.0	5.0
Folic Acid	mg/kg	0.8	0.8
Biotinh	mg/kg	0.07	0.07
Vitamin B12	mg/kg	0.02	0.02
Choline'	mg/kg	2400	2400

[a] Presumes an energy density of 4.0 kcaUg ME, based on the "modified Atwater" values of 3.5, 8.5, and 3.5 kcaVg for protein, fat, and carbohydrate (nitrogen-free extract, NFE), respectively. Rations greater than 4.5 kcaVg should be corrected for energy density; rations less than 4.0 kcaVg should not be corrected for energy.

[b] Although a true requirement for fat per se has not been established, the minimum level was based on recognition of fat as a source of essential fatty acids, as a carrier of fat-soluble vitamins, to enhance palatability, and to supply an adequate caloric density.

[c] If the mean urine pH of cats fed ad libitum is not below 6.4, the risk of struvite urolithiasis increases as the magnesium content of the diet increases.

[d] Because of very poor bioavailability, iron from carbonate or oxide sources that are added to the diet should not be considered as components in meeting the minimum nutrient level.

[e] Add 10 IU Vitamin E above minimum level per gram of fish oil per kilogram of diet.

[f] Vitamin K does not need to be added unless diet contains greater than 25% fish on a dry matter basis.

[g] Because processing may destroy up to 90% of the thiamine in the diet, allowances in formulation should be made to ensure the minimum nutrient level is met after processing.

[h] Biotin does not need to be added unless diet contains antimicrobial or antivitamin compounds.

[i] Methionine may substitute for choline as a methyl donor at a rate of 3.75 parts for 1 part choline by weight when methionine exceeds 0.62%.

The rationale for development of the nutrient profiles for cat foods can be found in the 1993 Official Publication starting on page 282.

MINIMUM PROTOCOL FOR USE IN THE DETERMINATION OF METABOLIZABLE ENERGY OF DOG AND CAT FOODS

METHOD 1: QUANTITATIVE COLLECTION

I. Animals

A minimum of six (6) fully grown animals at least one (1) year of age shall complete the test. The animals shall be in good health and of known weight. Animals shall be individually housed in metabolism cages. If urine is not collected and metabolizable energy is calculated based on correction factors for urine energy loss as specified in the protocol, protected covered runs may be used in lieu of metabolism cages.

II. Feeding Procedures

Feeding procedures shall be standardized. The feeding shall consist of two phases. The first phase shall be the pre-collection period of at least five (5) days with the objective of acclimating the test animals to the diet and adjusting food intake, as necessary, to maintain body weight. The second phase shall be the total collection period of at least five (5) days (120 hours). The amount of food offered during the second phase shall remain constant. Food intake shall be recorded throughout both phases.

III. Food

Food type, flavor, and production codes representing the composit feed shall be recorded. The food source shall remain constant throughout the test period.

IV. Food Allowances

The amount of food presented to each animal may be bases upon existing data on the quantity of food required to maintain body weight, or the estimated daily energy needs required for maintenance of various weights of dogs (Table 5, 1985 Nutrient Requirements of Dogs, NRC, or 132 kcal ME times body weight in kilograms to the 0.75 power) or cats (Table 4, 1986 Nutrient Requirements of Cats, NRC, or 70 kcal ME per kilogram body weight). Ad libitum feeding also may be used.

V. Times of Feeding

Animals shall be fed at least once daily and at the same time each day. Water shall be available at all times. Food shall be fed as is, or per normal feeding instructions for the product. The excess food shall be weighed back after the feeding.

VI. Pre-Trial Termination

If, during the pre-collection phase, the food is continually rejected or results in minimal consumption by a majority of the animals, the trial shall not proceed into the collection phase.

VII. Feces Collection

It is imperative that all collection containers be clearly marked using double labels. The labels shall include the animal number, diet number, and dates of collection. Feces shall be collected daily over 120 hours. Every effort should be made to collect all of the feces and avoid collecting hair. The methodology is as follows:

1. Weigh collection container and record weight.

2. Place feces in the respective animal's container for that day of collection. Collect feces as quantitatively as possible.

3. Place collections in freezer for storage.

4. Feces may be dried each day.

a. Weigh and record the weight of the feces and container each day, and determine net weight of feces. If the volume of feces is large, an aliquot may be retained for drying.

b. Dry daily feces collection (or aliquot). Feces should be thin enough to dry quickly. Otherwise, nitrogen and carbon losses may occur due to fermentation products.

c. Composite the entire 120-hour collection or proportional aliquots.

VIII. Sample Preparation

A. Food The food shall be blended to ensure a uniform consistency and an adequate quantity used for appropriate assays. Ample quantities of the remaining sample should be frozen and retained until assay results have been reviewed and found acceptable.

B. Feces shall be analyzed using composite samples. The samples shall be blended to ensure a uniform consistency and an adequate quantity used for appropriate assays. Ample quantities of the remaining sample should be frozen and retained until assay results have been reviewed and found acceptable.

C. Urine

IF urine collections are made, they shall be for the same period as the feces collections. Urine shall be collected, with a minimum of contamination in a urine receptacle containing sulfuric acid to stabilize the urine and prevent nitrogen loss. After the total urine volume is determined, aliquot samples shall be freeze-dried in an appropriate container.

IX. Analytical Determinations

Prepared samples shall be used for analysis. A.O.A.C. approved analytical methodology shall be used when available. Food, feces, and urine (if collected) shall be assayed for gross energy (bomb calorimetry). If urine is not collected, food and feces also shall be assayed for crude protein.

X. Calculation of Metabolizable Energy The determination is based on assays of the gross energy consumed, minus the energy in the feces and correction for energy lost in the urine (or energy lost in urine as determined by calorimetry). A. Without urine collection ME = [gross energy of food consumed - gross energy of feces collected {(grams protein consumed - grams protein in feces} X correction factor for energy lost in urine)]/amount of food consumed

$$\underline{ME(kcal/leg)=(a \times h) - (c \times d)= [(h \times e/SO! - (d \times f/l00!] \times g \times 1000}$$
$$b$$

Correction factor for energy lost in urine = 1.25 kcallg for dogs, 0.86 kcaUg for cats

Example:
a. gross energy of food = 4.35 kcal/g
b. amount of food consumed = 1250 g Pet Food Energy Protocol 141
c. gross energy of feces = 1.65 kcaUg
d. amount of feces collected = 600 g
e. protein in food = 24%
f. protein in feces = 9%
g. correction factor (dog) = 1.25 kcaUg

a X b = 4.35 X 1250 = 5437.5 kcal gross energy of food consumed

c X d = 1.65 X 600 = 990 kcal gross energy of feces collected
b X e/100 = 1250 X 24/100 = 300
g protein of food consumed
d X f/100 = 600 X 9/ 100 = 54 g protein in feces

$$(300 - 54) X 1.25 = 307.5 \text{ kcal energy lost in urine}$$
$$ME = \frac{(5437.5 - 990 - 307.5) X 1000}{1250}$$
$$= 3310 \text{ kcal ME/kg food}$$

B. With urine collection
ME = (gross energy of food consumed - gross energy of feces collected gross energy of urine collected)/amount of food consumed

$$ME(kcaSkg) = \frac{(a X b) - (c X d) - (e X f) X 1000}{b}$$

Example:
a. gross energy of food = 4.35 kcaUg
b. amount of food consumed = 1250 g
c. gross energy of feces = 1.65 kcaUg
d. amount of feces collected = 600 g
e. gross energy of urine = 0.25 kcaUml
f. volume of urine = 1230 ml

a X b = 4.35 X 1250 = 5437.5 kcal gross energy of food consumed c X d = 1.65 X 600 = 990 kcal gross energy of feces collected
e X f = 307.5 kcal gross energy of urine collected
$$ME = \frac{(5437.5 - 990) 307.5) X 1000}{1250}$$
$$= 3310 \text{ kcal ME/kg food}$$

METHOD 2: INDICATOR METHOD

I. Animals

A minimum of six (6) fully grown animals at least one (1) year of age shall complete the test. The animals shall be in good health and of known weight. Animals shall be individually housed.

II. Feeding Procedures

Feeding procedures shall be standardized. The feeding shall consist of two phases. The first phase shall be the pre-collection period of at least five (5) days with the objective of acclimating the test animals to the diet and adjusting food intake as necessary, to maintain body weight. The second phase shall be the collection period, during which aliquots of feces shall be collected from at least three separate days.

III. Food

Food type, flavor, and production codes representing the composite feed shall be recorded. The food source shall remain constant throughout the test period. Approximately 0.25% chromic oxide shall be uniformly mixed in a quantity of food sufficient to feed all animals for the duration of the precollection and collection periods. The chromic oxide should be of high quality and free of soluble chromium. Fisher Certified powder or equivalent is suitable. For dry diets, the chromic oxide powder should be premixed with a feed ingredient before incorporation into the diet. Although it possibly could be sprayed onto an extruded product, the uniformity of dispersion is questionable. For canned diets, the chromic oxide powder should be added as an aqueous slurry. To aid in dispersion, a small amount of liquid detergent should be added to the slurry. This should help overcome the hydrophobic nature of chromic oxide and its tendency to form balls in solution.

IV. Food Allowances

The amount of food presented to each animal may be based upon existing data on the quantity of food required to maintain body weight, or the estimated daily energy needs required for maintenance of various weights of dogs (Table 5, 1985 Nutrient Requirements of Dogs, NRC, or 132 kcal ME times body weight in kilograms to the 0.75 power) or cats (Table 4, 1986 Nutrient Requirements of Cats, NRC, or 70 kcal ME per kilogram body weight). Adlibitum feeding also may be used.

V. Times of Feeding

Animals shall be fed at least once daily and at the same time each day. Water should be available at all times. Food shall be fed as is, or per normal feeding instructions for the product. The excess food shall be weighed back after the feeding.

VI. Pre-Trial Termination

If, during the pre-collection phase, the food is continually rejected or results in minimal consumption by a majority of the animals, the trial shall not proceed into the collection phase.

VII. Feces Collection

It is imperative that all collection containers be clearly marked using double labels. The labels shall include the animal number, diet number, and dates of collection. Aliquots of feces from three separate days shall be collected. Every effort should be made to avoid collecting hair. The aliquots shall be dried and composited.

VIII. Sample Preparation

A. Food The food shall be blended to ensure a uniform consistency and an adequate quantity used for appropriate assays. Ample quantities of the remaining sample should be frozen and retained until assay results have been reviewed and found acceptable.

B. Feces The feces shall be analyzed using composite samples. The samples shall be blended to ensure a uniform consistency and an adequate quantity used for Pet Food Energy Protocol 143 appropriate assays. Ample quantities of the remaining sample should be frozen and retained until assay results have been reviewed and found acceptable.

IX. Analytical Determination

Prepared samples shall be used for analysis. A.O.A.C. approved analytical methodology shall be used when available. Food and feces shall be assayed for gross energy (bomb calorimetry), crude protein, and chromium. Food and feces should be analyzed for chromium by the same method. The preferred method of analysis is atomic absorption spectrophotometry.[1] Controlled sample digestion and oxidation of the chromic oxide to chromates is critical for reproducible results. Colorimetric analysis of chromium is less reproducible than atomic absorption spectrophotometry.

X. Calculation of Metabolizable Energy

The determination is based on assays of the gross energy consumed, minus the energy in the feces and correction for energy lost in the urine.

ME = digestible energy - [digestible protein X correction factor for energy lost in urine]

DE = 1- gross energy of feces X % Cr2Oz in food X gross energy of food gross energy of food X % Cr203 in feces

DP = 1- % protein in feces X 'S CrzOl in food X % protein in food % protein in food X % Cr203 in feces

Correction factor = 1.25 kcaUg for dogs, 0.86 kcaUg for cats

DE(kcaUg food) = [1- [(b X c)/(a X d)]] X a

DP(g digestible protein/g food) = [1- [(f X c!/(e X d!]] X e
                                                                        100

ME(kcaUkg food) = [DE - (DP X g)] X 1000

Example:
a. gross energy of food = 4.35 kcaUg
b. gross energy of feces = 1.65 kcaUg
c. percent chromic oxide in food = 0.25%
 d. percent chromic oxide in feces = 0.52%
e. protein in food = 24%
f. protein in feces = 9%
g. correction factor (dog) = 1.25 kcaUg protein digested

DE = [1- [(1.65 X 0.25)/(4.35 X 0.52)]] X 4.35
    = 3.56 kcaUg food
DP = [1- [(9 X 0.25!/(24 X 0.52!]] X 24
                100
= 0.197 g digestible protein/g food
ME = 3.56 - (0.197 X 1.25) X 1000
    = 3310 kcal ME/kg food

XI. Reference

[1] Arthur D. The determination of chromium in animal feed and excreta by atomic absorption spectrophotometry. Can Spect 1970; 15:134.

[2] Affiant is familiar with the requirements of official Pet Food Regulations PF2 (1) and (m) concerning label representations as to nutritional adequacy of dog and cat food products.

[3] The nutritional representation which appears on the label attached to this Afficavit has been substantiated by adequate testing, which testing was performed in accordance with the requirements established by the American Association of Feed Control Officials for such testing.

[4] The test results substantiating the representtion of nutritional adequacy appearing on the attached label have been conpleted and recorded and such results are on file.

AFFIDAVITS

(a) Affidavit of Pet Food Testing Protocol Completion.

_____ Affidavit_____for Animal Testing
   (Company Name)   (Number)

1. Affiant is the_____ of_____and
               (Title)   (Name of Company)

is duly authorized to make and execute this Affidavit for and on behalf of said company.

2. Affiant is familiar with the requirements of official Pet Food Regulations PF2 (1) and (m) concerning label representations as to nutritional adequacy of dog and cat food products.

3. The nutritional representation which appears on the label attached to this Affidavit has been substantiated by adequate testing, which testing was performed in accordance with the requirements established by the American Association of Feed Control Officials for such testing.

4. The test results substantiating the representation of nutritional adequacy appearing on the attached label have been completed and recorded and such

results are on file at_____ _____
                   Location of Records   Name of Company

By_____

Subscribed and sworn to before

                           (Title)

me this_____day of
_____,19_____

__ _____
          Notary Public

GUIDELINES FOR PET FOOD
LABEL REVIEW BY THE
AAFCO PET FOOD COMMITTEE

Label reviews are provided as a voluntary service of the Committee to AAFCO members and interested industry representatives. The following guidelines assist the Committee in the efficient distribution and review of labels and other material and must be followed unless different instructions are provided by the Committee management.

1. Each industry member or state of ficial desiring the opinion of the Committee regarding any printed labeling or printed material should contact the vice-chair and secure an official number and the names and addresses of each Committee member. The PFC number must be listed on all correspondence and printed material sent the Committee.

2. The label review package must include: a. Cover letter, b. Request for Pet Food Label Review form, c. Labels, and d. Affidavits for nutritional adequacy. The labels and other material in the label review package should reasonably represent the product material to be distributed with respect to color, style, placement, and type size. Labels should be 8 1/2" x 11" or attached to an 8 1/2" x 11" piece of paper; larger sized labels

will not be accepted. Faxed label review packages or labels will not be reviewed.

3. The Committee will try to complete the reviews within 45 calendar days of receipt of the material. Labels and issues submitted for discussion at a Pet Food Committee Meeting must be submitted at least 45 days prior to that meeting.

4. Polling of individual Committee members does not represent the informed opinion of the whole Committee. Individual committee members will not respond to requests for their opinion on pet food labeling issues unless the issue is submitted to the entire committee in the format described in these guidelines.

5. A state official is not bound by the recommendations of the Committee and may choose to act as authorized by that state's feed law/regulations. However, states are encouraged to accept the recommendations and interpretations of the Committee for the sake of uniformity.

Your cooperation in adhering to these guidelines will assist the Committee in continuing this review process.

REQUEST FOR PET FOOD LABEL REVIEW

Submitted by: _____ PFC Number _____

Address _____ Date _____

City, State Zip _____

Contact: _____

      Name   Title   Telephone Number

To be Reviewed: May Meeting August Meeting January Meeting By Mail New Product Change Other

CHECKLIST

1. Product Name
   - a. Based on PF Regulation:
   - b. Substantiation
2. Nutritional Claims
   - a. Complete and Balanced: (attach affidavit)
   - b. Other
3. Comparison Claims a. Substantiation
4. Ingredients not defined by AAFCO
5. Other Product Claims/Support
6. Attachments
7. Additional Comments
8. AAFCO Comments

Approved:

_____

Chairman

_____

Date

Note: If additional space is needed, use reverse side of this page. Labels for review should be submitted 45 days in advance.

Part 3.
Feed Ingredient Definitions

9. ANIMAL PRODUCTS
Investigator and Section Editor—Nancy Cook, VA

Official
9.2 **Meat** is the clean flesh derived from slaughtered mammals and is limited to that part of the striate muscle which is skeletal or that which is found in the tongue, in the diaphragm, in the heart, or in the esophagus; with or without the accompanying and overlying fat and the portions of the skin, sinew, nerve, and blood vessels which normally accompany the flesh. It shall be suitable for use in animal food. If it bears a name descriptive of its kind, it must correspond thereto. (Adopted 1938, Amended 1939, 1963.) IFN 5-00-394 Animal meat fresh

9.3 **Meat** by-products is the non-rendered, clean parts, other than meat, derived from slaughtered mammals. It includes, but is not limited to, lungs, spleen, kidneys, brain, livers, blood, bone, partially defatted low temperature fatty tissue, and stomachs and intestines freed of their contents. It does not include hair, horns, teeth and hoofs. It shall be suitable for use in animal food. If it bears name descriptive of its kind, it must correspond thereto. (Proposed 1973, Adopted 1974, Amended 1978) IFN 5-00-395 Animal meat by-products fresh

9.7 **Animal Liver** if it bears a name descriptive of its kind, it must correspond thereto. Meal is obtained by drying and grinding liver from slaughtered mammals. (Adopted 1954.) IFN 5-00-389 Animal livers meal

9.10 **Poultry By-Product Meal** consists of the ground, rendered, clean parts of the carcass of slaughtered poultry, such as necks, feet, undeveloped eggs, and intestines, exclusive of feathers, except in such amounts as might occur unavoidably in good processing practices. The label shall include guarantees for minimum crude protein, minimum crude fat, maximum crude fiber, minimum Phosphorus (P), and minimum and maximum calcium (Ca). The Calcium (Ca) level shall not exceed the actual level of phosphorus (P) by more than 2.2 times. (Proposed 1985, Adopted 1990) IFN 5-03-798 Poultry by-product meal rendered.

9.11 **Poultry Hatchery By-Product** is a mixture of egg shells, infertile and unhatched eggs, and culled chicks which have been cooked, dried, and ground, with or without removal of part of the fat. (Adopted 1957.) I IFN 5-03-796 Poultry hatchery by-product meal

9.12 **Dried Meat Solubles** is obtained by drying the defatted water extract of the clean, wholesome parts of slaughtered animals prepared by steaming or hot water extraction. It must be designated according to its crude protein content which shall be no less than 70%. (Proposed 1961, Adopted 1962, Amended 1964,1967.) , IFN 5-00-393 Animal meat solubles dehydrated

9.14 **Poultry By-Products** must consist of non-rendered clean parts of carcasses of slaughtered poultry such as heads, feet, viscera, free from fecal content and foreign matter except in such trace amounts as might occur unavoidably in good factory practice. (Proposed 1963, Adopted 1964.) IFN 5-03-800 Poultry by-product fresh

9.15 **Hydrolyzed Poultry Feathers** is the product resulting from the treatment under pressure of dean, undecomposed feathers from slaughtered poultry, free of additives, and/or accelerators. Not less than 75% of its crude protein content must be digestible by the pepsin digestibility method.* (Proposed 1961, Adopted 1965.) IFN 5-03-795 Poultry feathers meal hydrolyzed

9.16 **Fleshings Hydrolysate** is obtained by acid hydrolysis of the flesh from fresh or salted hides. It is defatted, strained, and neutralized. If evaporated to 50% solids, it shall be designated Condensed Fleshings Hydrolysate." It must have a minimum crude protein and maximum salt guarantee. (Proposed 1967, Adopted 1968.) Reg. 573.200 ION 5-08 094 Animal skin fleshings hydrolyzed rendered

9.40 **Meat Meal** is the rendered product from mammal tissues, exclusive of any added blood, hair, hoof, horn, hide trimmings, manure, stomach and rumen contents except in such amounts as may occur unavoidably in good processing practices. It shall not contain added extraneous materials not provided for by this definition. The Calcium (Ca) level shall not exceed the actual level of Phosphorus (P) by more than 2.2 times. It shall not contain more than 12% Pepsin indigestible residue and not more than 9% of the crude protein in the product shall be pepsin indigestible*. The label shall in-clude guarantees for minimum crude protein, minimum crude fat, maximum crude fiber, minimum Phosphorus (P) and minimum and maximum Calcium (Ca). If the product bears a name descriptive of its kind, composition or origin, it must correspond thereto. (Proposed 1971, Adopted 1972, Amended 1985, Adopted 1993.) IFN 5-00-385 Animal meat meal rendered.

9.41 **Meat and Bone Meal** is the rendered product from mammal tissues, including bone, exclusive of any added blood, hair, hoof, horn, hide trimmings, manure, stomach and rumen contents, except in such amounts as may occur unavoidably in good processing practices. It shall not contain added extraneous materials not provided for in this definition. It shall contain a minimum of 4.0% Phosphorus (P) and the Calcium (Ca) level shall not be more than 2.2 times the actual Phosphorus (P) level. It shall not contain more than 12% pepsin indigestible residue* and not more than 9% of the crude protein in the product shall be pepsin indigestible*. The label shall include guarantees for minimum crude protein, minimum crude fat, maximum crude fiber, minimum Phosphorus (P) and minimum and maximum Calcium (Ca). If it bears a name description of its kind, composition or origin it must correspond thereto. (Proposed 1985, Amended 1992, Adopted 1994.) ~ 4 ICON 5~388 Animal meat with bone rendered.

9.42 **Animal By-Product Meal** is the rendered product from animal tissues, exclusive of any added hair, hoof, horn, hide trimmings, manure, stomach and rumen contents, except in such amounts as may occur unavoidably in good processing practices. It shall not contain added extraneous materials not I provided for by this definition. This ingredient definition is intended to cover | those individual rendered animal tissue products that cannot meet the criteria as set forth elsewhere in this section. This ingredient is not intended to be used to label a mixture of animal tissue products. (Proposed 1985, Amended X 1992, Adopted 1993.) / IFN S-08-786.

9.50 **Meat Meal Tankage** is the rendered product from mammal tissues, exclusive of any added hair, hoof, horn, hide trimmings, manure, stomach and: rumen contents, except in such amounts as may occur unavoidably in processing factory practices. It may contain added blood or blood meal, however, it shall not contain any other added extraneous materials not provided for by this definition. The Calcium (Ca) level shall not exceed the actual level of Phosphorus (P) by more than 2.2 times. It shall not contain more than 12% pepsin indigestible residue and not more than 9% of the crude protein in product shall be pepsin indigestible*. The label shall include guarantees for minimum crude protein, minimum crude fat, maximum crude fiber, minimum Phosphorus (P) and minimum and maximum Calcium (Ca). If the product bears a name descriptive of its kind, composition or origin it must correspond thereto. (Proposed 1985, Amended 1992, Adopted 1994.) IFN 5-00-386 Animal tankage meal rendered.

9.51 **Meat and Bone Meal Tankage** is the rendered product from mammal tissues, including bone, exclusive of any added hair, hoof, horn, hide trimmings, manure, stomach and rumen contents except in such amounts as may occur unavoidably in good processing practices. It may contain added blood or blood meal, however, it shall not contain any added extraneous materials not provided for in this definition. . It shall contain a minimum of 4.0% Phosphorus (P) and the Calcium (Ca) level shall not be more than 2.2 times the actual Phosphorus (P) level. It shall not contain more than 12% pepsin indigestible residue and not more than 9% of the crude protein in the product shall be pepsin indigestible*. The label shall include guarantees for minimum crude protein, minimum crude fat, maximum crude fiber, minimum Phosphorus (P) and minimum and maximum Calcium (Ca). If the product bears a name descriptive of its kind, composition or origin it must correspond thereto. (Proposed 1985, Adopted 1994.) IFN 5-00-387 Animal tankage with bone rendered.

9.54 **Hydrolyzed Hair** is a product prepared from clean, undecomposed hair, by heat and pressure to produce a product suitable for animal feeding Not less than 80% of its crude protein must be digestible by the pepsin digestibility method* (Proposed 1968, Adopted 1970.) IFN 5-08-997 Animal hair hydrolyzed Oh

9.55 **Hydrolyzed Leather Meal** is produced from leather scrap that is treated with steam for not less than 33 minutes at a pressure not less than 125 pounds per square inch and further processed to contain not more than 10% moisture, not less than 60% crude protein, not more than 6% crude fiber, not more than 2.75% chromium, and with not less than 80% of its crude protein digestible by the pepsin digestibility method*. Hydrolyzed leather meal may be utilized in livestock feeds as provided in food additive regulation 573.540 (Proposed 1968, Adopted 1970.) IFN 5-08-998 Animal leather meal hydrolyzed

9.56 **Spray Dried Animal Blood** is produced from clean, fresh animal blood, exclusive of all extraneous material such as hair, stomach belching, urine, except in such traces as might occur unavoidably in good factory practice. Moisture is removed from the blood by a low temperature, evaporator under vacuum until it contains approximately 30% solids. It is then dried by spraying into a draft of warm, dry air which reduces the blood to finely divided particles with a maximum moisture of 8% and a minimum crude protein of 85%. It must be designated according to its minimum water solubility. (Proposed 1972, Amended 1976, Adopted 1978.) IFN 5-00-381 Animal blood spray dehydrated

9.60 **Egg Shell Meal** is mixture of egg shells, shell membranes and egg content obtained by drying the residue from an egg breaking plant in a dehydrator to an end product temperature of 180(f48)L(fl3)F. It must be designated according to its protein and calcium content.(Prop. 1975,Adopted 1982) g IFN 6-26-004 Poultry egg shells meal

9.61 **Blood Meal** is produced from clean, fresh animal blood, exclusive of all extraneous materials such as hair, stomach belchings and urine, except as might occur unavoidably in good processing practices. The process used must be listed as a part of the product name such as conventional cooker dried, steamed or hydrolyzed. The product usually has a dark black like color and is rather insoluble in water. (Proposed 1975, Adopted 1979, Amended 1991, Adopted 1993). IFN 5-26-005 Animal blood meal conventional cooker dehydrated IFN Number _ Animal blood meal steamed dehydrated s IFN Number _ Animal blood meal hydrolyzed dehydrated,

9.62 **Blood Meal**, Flash Dried is produced from clean, fresh animal blood, exclusive of all extraneous material such as hair, stomach belchings and urine except as might occur unavoidably in good manufacturing processes. A large portion of the moisture (water) is usually removed by a mechanical dewatering process or by condensing by cooking to a semi-solid state. The semi-solid blood mass is then transferred to a rapid drying facility where the more tightly bound water is rapidly removed. The minimum biological activity of Lysine shall be 80%. (Proposed 1975, Adopted 1980.) IFN 5-26-006 Animal blood meal flash dehydrated

9.63 **Blood Protein** is produced by quick freezing and/or transporting in a chilled state, clean, fresh, whole or dewatered animal blood exclusive of all extraneous material such as hair, stomach belchings and urine except as might occur unavoidably in good manufacturing processes. If the product bears a name descriptive of its kind, composition or origin, it must correspond thereto. (Proposed 1975, Amended 1980, Adopted 1982, Amended 1993, Adopted 1994.) IFN 5-25-007 Animal blood fresh

9.65 **Glandular Meal and Extracted Glandular Meal** is obtained by drying liver and other glandular tissues from slaughtered mammals. When a significant portion of the water soluble material has been removed, it may be called Extracted Glandular Meal. (Proposed 1979, Adopted 1980.) IFN 5-12-247 Animal glands meal IFN 5-30-080 Animal glands meal water extracted

9.67 **Unborn Calf Carcasses** is the product obtained from whole unborn carcasses taken from slaughtered cows at government inspected slaughter plants. The product is produced by grinding the whole unborn carcass, exclusive of calf hides. The product is denatured, fresh frozen and shall be suitable for use as an animal feed. (Proposed 1979, Adopted 1980.) -I IFN 5-30-081 Cattle fetus carcass without skin

9.68 **Animal Digest** is a material which results from chemical and/or enzymatic hydrolysis of clean and undecomposed animal tissue. The animal tissues used shall be exclusive of hair, horns, teeth, hooves and feathers, except in such trace amounts as might occur unavoidably in good factory practice and shall be suitable for animal feed. If it bears a name descriptive of its kind or flavor(s), it must correspond thereto. (Proposed 1981, Amended 1983, Adopted 1990) IFN 5~935 Animal Digest Condensed.

9.69 **Cooked Bone Marrow** is the soft material coming from the center of large bones, such as leg bones. This material, which is predominantly fat with some protein, must be separated from the bone material by cooking with steam. It shall not contain added extraneous materials not provided for by this definition except for small amount of tissue which may adhere to the bone unavoidably in good processing practice. The labeling of this product shall include, but is not limited to, guarantees for minimum crude protein and minimum crude fat. (Proposed 1988, Adopted 1992)

9.70 **Mechanically Separated Bone Marrow** is the soft material coming from the center of large bones, such as leg bones. This material, which is predominantly fat with some protein, must be separated from the bone material by mechanical separation. It shall not contain added extraneous materials not provided for by this definition except for small amount of tissue which may adhere to the bone unavoidably in good processing practice. The labeling of this product shall include, but is not limited to, guarantees for minimum crude protein and minimum crude fat. (Proposed 1988, Adopted 1992)

9.71 **Poultry Meal** is the dry rendered product from a combination of clean flesh and skin with or without accompanying bone, derived from the parts of whole carcasses of poultry or a combination thereof, exclusive of feathers, heads, feet, and entrails. It shall be suitable for use in animal food. If it bears a name descriptive of its kind, it must correspond thereto. (Proposed 1988+ Adopted 1992)

9.72 **Animal Plasma** is the product obtained by spray drying plasma which has been separated away from the cellular matter (red and white blood cells) of fresh whole blood by chemical and mechanical processing. The protein portion of this product is primarily albumin, globulin, and fibrinogen type proteins. The minimum percent crude protein and the maximum percent ash must be guaranteed on the label. If it bears a name descriptive of its kind, composition, or origin, it must correspond thereto. (Proposed 1990, Adopted 1993)

9.73 **Ensiled Paunch Product** is a product composed of the contents of rumen of cattle slaughtered at USDA inspected facilities. The moisture level is reduced to 50-68%. The product is then packed into an airtight environment, such as a silo, where it undergoes an acid fermentation that retards spoilage. The ensiled product will have a Ph of 4.0 or less. (Proposed 1990, Adopted 1992)

9.75 **Leather Hydrolyzate** is obtained from leather trimmings that are pressure cooked with the addition of steam and sodium hydroxide. Chromium is precipitated and separated so that not over 30 ppm (SOLIDS BASIS) remain - in the hydrolyzate. This product can be used as a liquid ingredient or as a powder. In either event, the analysis on a solids basis will not be less than 75% crude protein and not less than 85% of the protein shall be pepsin digestible*. (Adopted 1993)

9.77 **Stock** is obtained by steam cooking USDA edible, fresh, wholesome bones containing meat and muscle tissue at least 3 hours at a minimum temperature of 180 F and then drying the extracted broth. It must be designated as edible and according to its crude protein content which shall not be less than 90%. In order for a reconstituted product to be labeled as stock, the moisture-to-protein ratio must not exceed 135:1 (135 parts water to 1 part protein). If the product bears a name descriptive of its kind, composition or origin, it must correspond thereto. (Proposed 1993, Adopted 1994.)

9.78 **Meat Protein Isolate** is produced by separating meat protein from fresh, clean, unadulterated bones by heat processing followed by low temperature drying to preserve function and nutrition. This product is characterized by a fresh meaty aroma, a 90% minimum protein level, 1% maximum fat and 2% maximum ash. (Proposed 1993, Adopted 1994.)
*Determined by AOAC method listed in the Check Sample Reference for Analytical Variations.

Tentative

T957 **Poultry** is the clean combination of flesh and skin with or without accompanying bone, derived from the parts or whole carcasses of poultry or a combination thereof, exclusive of feathers, heads, feet and entrails. It shall be suitable for use in animal food. If it bears a name descriptive of its kind, it must correspond thereto. If the bone has been removed, the process may be so designated by use of the appropriate feed term. (Proposed 1978, Adopted 1979, Amended 1995)

T958 **Hydrolyzed Whole Poultry** is the product resulting from the hydrolyzation of whole carcasses of culled or dead, undecomposed, poultry including: feathers, heads, feet, entrails, undeveloped eggs, blood and any other specific portions of the carcass.

The product must be consistent with the actual proportions of whole poultry and must be free of added parts; including, but not limited to entrails, blood or feathers. The poultry may be fermented as a part of the manufacturing process. The product shall be processed in such a fashion as to make it suitable for animal food, including heating (boiling at 212 F, or 100 C at sea level, for 30 minutes, or its equivalent, and agitated, except in steam cooking equipment). The product may if acid treated, be subsequently neutralized. If the product bears a name descriptive of its kind, the name must correspond thereto. (Proposed 1995)

T959 **Hydrolyzed Poultry By-Products** Aggregate is the product resulting from hydrolyzation, heat treatment, or a combination thereof, of all byproducts of slaughter poultry, clean and undecomposed, including such parts as heads, feet, undeveloped eggs, intestines, feathers and blood. The parts may be fermented as a part of the manufacturing process. The product shall be processed in such a fashion as to make it suitable for animal food, including heating (boiling at 212 F, or 100 C at sea level for 30 minutes, or its equivalent, and agitated, except in steam cooking equipment). It may, if acid treated, be subsequently neutralized. If the product bears a name descriptive of its kind, the name must correspond thereto. (Proposed 1978, Adopted 1980 Amended 1995)

T9.74 **Egg Product** is product obtained

from egg graders, egg breakers and/or hatchery operations that is dehydrated, handled as liquid, or frown These shall be labeled as per USDA regulations governing eggs and egg products (7CFR, Part 59). This product shall be free of shells or other non-egg materials except in such amounts which might occur unavoidably in good processing practices, and contain a maximum ash content of 6% on a dry mat ter basis. (Proposed 1991, Amended 1994).

75. RICE PRODUCTS
Investigator and Section Editor- Jamey Johnson AR Official

75.1 Rice Polishings is a by-product of rice obtained in the milling operation of brushing the grain to polish the kernel. (Adopted 1938.) IFN 4-03-943 Rice polishings

75.2 Ground Rough Rice or Ground Paddy is the entire product obtained in grinding the whole rice grain including the hulls. (Adopted prior to 1928, Amended 1959.) IFN 4-03-938 Rice grain ground

75.3 Rice Bran, Solvent Extracted is obtained by removing part of the oil from rice bran by the use of solvents and must contain not less than 14% crude protein and not more than 14% crude fiber. (Adopted 1951, Amended 1959.) w IFN 4-03-930 Rice bran with germ meal solvent extracted -,:

75.4 Chipped Rice, Broken Rice, or Brewers Rice is the small fragments of rice kernels that have been separated from the larger kernels of milled rice. (Proposed 1959, Adopted 1960.) IFN 4-03-932 Rice groats polished broken

75.5 **Ground Brown Rice** is the entire product obtained in grinding the rice kernels after the hulls have been removed. (Proposed 1959, Adopted 1960.) IFN 4-03-935 Rice groats ground

75.6 **Rice Hulls** consists primarily of the outer covering of the rice. (Proposed 1959, Adopted 1960.) IFN 1-08-075 Rice hubs

75.7 **Rice Bran** is the pericarp or bran layer and germ of the rice, with only such quantity of hub fragments, chipped, broken, or brewers rice, and calcium carbonate as is unavoidable in the regular mining of edible rice. It must contain not more than 13% crude fiber. When the calcium carbonate exceeds 3% (Ca.-1.2%), the percentage must be declared in the brand name; i.e., Rice Bran with-Calcium Carbonate not exceeding _ %. (Proposed 1963, Adopted 1964.) f IFN 4-03-928 Rice bran with germs

75.8 **Rice Mill By-Product** is the total offal obtained in the mining of nce. It Consists of rice hubs, rice bran, rice polishings and broken rice grains. Its crude fiber content must not exceed 32%. (Proposed 1961, Adopted 1965.)] IFN 1~941 Rice mid run NOTE: See also 87.6 and 87.7

Tentative
T759 **Parboiled Rice Bran** is about to 7%

by weight of Parboiled Rough Rice and is a mixture made up of a combination of several botanical tissues: pericarp, seed coat, nucellus, and the outermost portion of the endosperm (the aleurone layer). It may contain hull fragments, broken grains and traces of added calcium carbonate as is unavoidable in the milling of parboiled rice. (Proposed 1992)

T75.10 **Stabilized Rice Bran** is rice bran which has been treated soon after milling by heat or other means that will substantially reduce the lipase activity. Free fatty acid content of the crude fat extracted shall not exceed four percent.   (AOAC940-28) (Proposed 1995)

Part 4. Additives & GRAS
(Generally Recognized As Safe) Substances

The following list of Least Common Feed Ingredients, although not defined specifically by AAFCO, are listed in the U.S. Code of Federal Regulations as food additives (21 CFR 573) or as generally recognized as safe (GRAS) ingredients (21 CFR 582). The CFR reference is cited and should be consulted for full information concerning their uses and restrictions.

Please note that only those ingredients that are not defined appear in the following lists.

PART 573-FOOD ADDITIVES PERMITTED IN FEED AND DRINKING WATER OF ANIMALS

573.120 Acrylamide-acrylic acid resin.

573.440 Ethylene dichloride.

573.530 Hydrogenated corn syrup.

573.740 Odorless light petroleum hydrocarbons.

573.880 Normal propyl alcohol.

573.1010 Xanthan gum.

PART 582—SUBSTANCES GENERALLY REC-OGNIZED AS SAFE IN ANIMAL FEEDS
Subpart B General Purpose Food Additives

Section

582.80 Copper pyrophosphate

582.1005 Acetic acid.

582.1009 Adipic acid.

582.1057 Hydrochloric acid.

582.1061 Lactic acid.

582.1069 Malic acid.

582.1077 Potassium acid tartrate.

582.1087 Sodium acid pyrophosphate.

582.1091 Succinic acid.

582.1095 Sulfuric acid.

582.1099 Tartaric acid.

582.1127 Aluminum ammonium sulfate.

582.1129 Aluminum potassium sulfate.

582.1131 Aluminum sodium sulfate.

582.1135 Ammonium bicarbonate.

582.1137 Ammonium carbonate.

582.1139 Ammonium hydroxide.

582.1165 Butane.

582.1195 Calcium citrate.

582.1207 Calcium lactate.

582.1235 Caramel.

582.1240 Carbon dioxide.

582.1275 Dextrans.

582.1320 Glycerin.

582.1324 Glyceryl monostearate.

582.1355 Helium.

582.1366 Hydrogen peroxide.

582.1480 Methylcellulose.

582.1500 Monoammonium glutamate.

582.1516 Monopotassium glutamate.

582.1540 Nitrogen.

582.1585 Papain.

582.1655 Propane.

582.1685 Rennet.

582.1711 Silica aerogel.

582.1721 Sodium acetate

582.1748 Sodium caseinate.

582.1751 Sodium citrate.

582.1763 Sodium hydroxide.

582.1775 Sodium pectinate.

582.1781 Sodium aluminum phosphate.

582.1804 Sodium potassium tartrate.

582.1901 Triacetin.

582.1973 Beeswax.

582.1975 Bleached beeswax.

582.1978 Carnauba wax.

Subpart C-Anti-caking Agents

Section

582.2122 Aluminum calcium silicate.

582.3225 Calcium sorbate

582.2437 Magnesium silicate.

582.3336 Gum guaiac

582.2729 Hydrated sodium calcium aluminosilicate.

582.2906 Tricalcium silicate

Subpart F-Nutrients and/or Dietary Supplements

Section

582.5017 Aspartic acid.

582.5049 Aminoacetic acid.

582.5065 Linoleic acid.

582.5118 Alanine.

582.5145 Arginine.

582.5195 Calcium citrate.

582.5201 Calcium glycerophosphate.

582.5223 Calcium pyrophosphate.

582.5250 Choline bitartrate.

582.5271 Cysteine. 582.5273 Cystine.

582.5306 Ferric sodium pyrophosphate.

5825311 Ferrous lactate.

5825361 Histidine.

582.5370 Inositol.

582.5381 Isoleucine.

582.5406 Leucine.

582.5455 Manganese glycerophosphate.

582.5458 Manganese hypophosphite.

582.5470 Mannitol.

582.5580 D-Pantothenyl alcohol.

582.5590 Phenylalanine.

582.5628 Potassium glycerophosphate

582.5650 Proline.

582.5676 Pyridoxine hydrochloride.

5825697 Riboflavin-5-phosphate.

5825701 Serine.

582.5772 Sodium pantothenate.

582.5778 Sodium phosphate

5825835 Sorbitol.

5825920 Tyrosine.

582.5925 Valine.

582.5930 Vitamin A

582.5950 Vitamin D2

582.5988 Zinc gluconate.

582.5994 Zinc sterate.

Subpart G-Sequestrants

582.6033 Citric acid.

582.6085 Sodium acid phosphate.

582.6099 Tartaric acid.

582.6185 Calcium acetate.

582.6195 Calcium citrate.

582.6197 Calcium diacetate.

582.6203 Calcium hexametaphosphate.

582.6219 Calcium phytate.

582.6285 Dipotassium phosphate.

582.6386 Isopropyl citrate.

582.6511 Monoisopropyl citrate.

582.6751 Sodium citrate.

582.6754 Sodium diacetate.

582.6757 Sodium gluconate.

582.6769 Sodium metaphosphate.

582.6787 Sodium pyrophosphate.

582.6801 Sodium tartrate.

582.6804 Sodium potassium tartrate.

582.6807 Sodium thiosudate.

582.6851 Stearyl citrate.

Subpart H-Stabilizers

582.7115 Agar-agar.

582.7133 Ammonium alginate.

582.7187 Calcium alginate.

582.7330 Gum arabic.

582.7333 Gum ghatti.

582.7339 Guar gum.

582.7343 Locust bean gum.

582.7349 Sterculia gum.

582.7351 Gum tragacanth.

582.7610 Potassium alginate.

582.7724 Sodium alginate.

58210 Spices and other natural seasonings and flavorings.

Allspice
Angelica
Angelica seed
Hyssop
Licorice
Mace
Marjoram, pot
Balm (lemon balm)
Basil, sweet
Bay
Calendula

Ambrette seed
Angelica root
Horseradish
Lavender
Linden flowers
Marigold, pot
Angostura (cuspana bark)
Basil, bush
Marjoram, sweet
Mustard, black or brown
Mustard, brown

Camomile(chamomile),English,or Roman
Camomile(chamomile)German/Hungarian
Capers
Caraway, black (black cumin)
Cassia, Chinese Cassia, Padang or Batavia
Cayenne pepper
Chevril
Cinnamon, Ceylon
Cinnamon, Saigon
Clover
Coriander
Cumin, black (black caraway)
Elder flowers
Garlic
Glycyrrhiza
Horehound (hoarhound)
Mexican oregano, Mexican sage, origan)
Parsley
cayenne Pepper, red Pepper, white Peppermint
Pot marigold
Rosemary
Sage Sage,
Savory, winter
Spearmint
Tarragon
Tyme, wild or creeping
Vanilla

Mustard, white or yellow
Nutmeg
Caraway
Cardamorn (cardamon)
Cassia, Saigon
Celery seed
Chives
Cinnamon, Chinese
Clary (clary sage)
Cloves
Cumin (cummin)
Dill
Galanga (galangal)
Geramium
Grains of paradise
Oregano (origanum,
Paprika
Pepper, black Pepper,
Poppy Seed
Pot marjoram
Rue Saffron
Greek Savory, summer
Sesame
Star anise
Thyme
Tumeric
Zedoary

58220 Essential oils, oleroresins (solvent-free), and natural extractives (including distillates).

Alfalfa
Almond, bitter (free from prussic acid)
Angelica root
Angelica stem
Amse
Balsalm of Peru
Bay leaves
Bergamot (bergamot orange)

Geranium, rose
Glycyrrhiza

Allspice
Ambrette (seed)
Angelica seed
Angostura (cuspana bark)
Asafetida Balm (lemon balm)
Basil
Bay (myrcia oil)
Bitter almond (free from prussic acid)
Bois de rose (hnger Cacao
Camomile (chamomile) flowers,

Hungarian
Camomile (chamomile) flowers,
Roman or English
Cananga
Caraway
Carob bean
Cascarila bark
Cassia bark, Padang or Batavia
Celery seed
Chervil
Cinnamon bark,
Cinnamon bark, Chinese
Cinnamon bark, Ceylon
Cinnamon leaf, Saigon
Citrus peels
Clove bud
Clove stem
Coffee
Coriander
Cumin (cummin)

Cusparia bark
Dandelion root
Dog grass (quackgrass, triticum)
Estragole (esdragol, esdragon,
        tarragon)
Fennel, sweet
Galanga (galangal)
Geranium
Horehound (hoarhound)
Hyssop
Jasmine
Kola nut
Laurel leaves
Lavender, spike
Lemon
Lemon grass
Licorice Lime
Locust bean
Mace
Mandarin
Male 1
Menthol
Molasses (extract)
Naringin
Nutmeg
Orange, bitter, flowers
Orange leaf

Grapefruit

Guava Hickory bark
Capsicum
Cardamom seed (cardamon)
Carrot
Cassia bark, Chinese
Cassia bark, Saigon
Cherry, wild, bark
Chicory
Ceylon
Cinnamon bark, Saigon
Cinnamon leaf, Chinese
Citronella
Clary (clary sage)
Clove leaf
Clover Coca (decocainized)
Cola nut
Corn silk
Curacao orange peel (orange,
        bitter peel)
Dandelion
Dill
Elder flowers

Estragon (tarragon)
Fenugreek
Garlic
Geranium, East Indian
Hops Horsemint
Immortelle
Juniper (berries)
Laurel berries
Lavender
Lavandin
Lemon balm (see balm)
Lemon peel
Linden flowers
Lupulin
Malt (extract)
Majoram, sweet
Melissa (see balm)
Menthyl acetate
Mustard
Neroli, bigarade
Onion
Orange, bitter, pe
Orange, sweet

Orange, sweet, flowers
Origanum
Paprika
Pepper, black Pepper, white
Peruvian balsam
Petitgrain lemon
Pimenta
Pipsissewa leaves
Prickly ash bark
Rose (otto of roses, attar of roses)
Rose flowers
Rose geranium
Rosemary
Saffron
Sage, Creek Sage, Spanish
Savory, summeri
Sloe berries (blackthorn berries)
Spike lavender
Tangerine
Tarragon Tea
Thyme, white
Tritcum (see dog grass)
Turmeric
Violet flowers
Violet leaves absolute
Yiang-yiang

Orange, sweet, peel
Palmarosa
Parsley
Peppermint
Petitgrain
Petitgrain mandarin or tangerine
Pimenta leaf
Pomegranate
Rose absolute
Rose buds
Rose Quit (hips)
Rose leaves
Rue
Sage
St. John's bread
Savory, winter
Spearmint
Tamarind
Tannic acid
Thyme
Thyme, wild or creeping
Tuberose
Vanilla
Violet leaves
Wild cherry bark
Zeodary bark

582.30 Natural substances used in conjunction with spices and other natural seasonings and flavorings.

Algae, brown (kelp)
Algae, red
Dulse

582.40 Natural extractives (solvent-free) used in conjunction with spices, seasonings, and flavorings

Algae, brown
Algae, red

Apricot kernel (persic oil)
Dulse Kelp (sea algae,brown)
Peach kernal (persic oil)
Peanut stearine
Persic oil (see apricot kernel and peach kernel)
Quince seed

582.50 Certain other spices, seasonings, essential oils, oleoresins, and natural extacts.

Ambergris
Castioreum
Civet (zibeth, zibet, zibetum)
Cognac oil, white and green
Musk(Tonquin musk)

582.60 Syntheic flavoring substances and adjuvants.

Acetaldehyde (ethanal).
Acetoin (acetyl methylcarbinol).
Aconitic acid (equisetic acid, citridic acid, achilleic acid).
Anethole (parapropenyl anisole).
Benzaldehyde (benzoic aldehyde).
N-Butyric acid (butanoic acid).
d-or l-Carvone (carvol).
Cinnamaldehyde (cinnamic aldehyde).
Decanal (N-decylaldehyde, capraldehyde, capric aldehyde, caprinaldehyde, aldehyde (C-10).
Diacetyl (2,3-butandeione).
Ethyl acetate.
Ethyl butyrate.
3-Methyl-3-phenyl glycidic acid ethyl ester (ethyl-methyl-phenyl-glycidate, so called strawberry aldehyde, C-16 aldehyde).
Ethyl vanillin.
Eugenol.
Geranoil (3,7-dimethyl-2,6 and 3,6-octadien-l-ol).

Geranyl acetate (geraniol acetate).

Glycerol (glyceryl) tributyrate (tributyrin, butyrin).

Limonene (d-, I-, and di-).

Linalool (linalol, 3,7-dimethyl-1,6-octadien-(3-ol).

Linalyl acetate (bergamol).

1-Malic acid.

Methyl anthranilate (methyl-2-aminobenzoate).

Piperonal (3,4-methylenedioxy-benzaldehyde-heliotropin).

Vanillin.

Chapter Five

CANCER - CHEMICALS AND POISONS

On a visit to Africa I was amazed to find the incidence of cancer among indigenous natives non-existent. Why? Their diets consist of all natural foods. Today, five cultures on earth live to be 120-140 years old. These people from parts of Russia, China, Ecuador, and Peru all have commonalities. They live in valleys above 8,000 feet and their food and water is highly mineralized naturally from glaciers. Their food is totally organic, the air is clean, pure, and chemicals are non-existent.

Chemicals Produce Cancer....Yet our government agencies continue to allow their usage. In the early 1990's the F.D.A. admitted 71 agricultural chemicals cause cancer.

In 1990 my father passed away after several months of treatment for cancer. The physician responsible for the treatment admitted there is no cure for cancer only treatment. Often times the patient dies from the treatment rather than the disease. Who knows how long my father would have lived had he not been treated. I know his quality of life would have been far better than the misery he experienced.

Cancer Can Be Prevented In Animals and Humans. My research with English Setters has clearly proven how to prevent cancer through nutrition. We live in the most technologically advanced country in the world and have the highest incidence of cancer in the universe. The answer to preventing this dreaded disease is at our fingertips. The facts clearly support the theory that Cancer is directly related to chemicals. Doesn't it seem ironic that in hundreds of countries around the globe there is *no incidence of cancer* and these countries have little or no usage of chemicals?

Our country is literally drowning in chemicals and everyone seems content to march on, complacent and satisfied with the status-quo, with no concerns for tomorrow. It is nearly impossible to go through just one day without consuming chemicals in our water, the soda beverages we drink, the food we eat, even the shampoo we wash with and the air we breathe. Everywhere you look there are hazardous chemicals in our kitchen cabinets, garages and closets. All have dangerous warning labels; yet we use them with reckless abandon.

During a discussion of chemicals with a Neurologist, he informed me that sixty percent of his practice was devoted to treating patients for migraine headaches. Over half of these patients' problems were cured by simply eliminating all canned foods from their diet. A chemical preservative in many canned products is the culprit.

It has been proven that the top ten causes of death are directly related to nutrition. Like veterinariary schools, less than 40 percent of medical schools in Canada and the U.S. offer the minimum hours (only 25) of nutrition training. According to a 1993 article in SELF magazine, more than 75 percent of medical schools do not require students to take a single nutrition course.

Chemicals poison our rivers and streams, the air we breathe, the food we eat. All this is with government approval. Not one species of insects has been eradicated through the use of chemical pesticides. Only two-thirds of the insects are killed when sprayed and each year; thereafter, new chemicals must be formulated to prevent insects from becoming tolerant specific.

The Southwestern United States is being inundated by fire ants. These ants threaten both wildlife and domestic animals alike. On our ranch in Texas new mounds of fire ants are being discovered almost daily. I have experimented with every chemical fire ant poison available. In every case it appears the ant mound has been killed out; however, in a few weeks many of those same mounds begin rebuilding with fireants. At the very best it appears that these chemicals are only killing a portion of the ants, and I would discourage the use of any of these poisons.

In 1996 the U.S. Environmental Protection Agency, that government body looking out for our well being, has gone on record as saying, "Several large Texas cities have dangerous levels of the chemical Diazinon in storm water run-off." They want the cities to develop a method to treat this water, regardless of the expense! The solution to this problem is simple, ban Diazinon. This is a toxic, dangerous chemical. At the very least it's use should be restricted.

A friend of mine is the Manager of Environmental Services for the state of Texas. His job consists of obtaining water samples from the lakes, rivers, and tributaries that make up the water supply for metropolitan areas in the state. These water samples show toxicity from years and years of chemical spraying. Many of the lakes and reservoirs in East Texas are contaminated with arsenic.

"Arsenic compound" has been used as a defoliate for cotton up until the 70's and 80's. It was sprayed upon cotton fields to kill the leaves prior to picking the cotton. Over the years, the arsenic has accumulated in the fields, and due to its tendency to attach to the soil, it is picked up and transported by runoff from rainfall events. The material is then transported down the streams into our reservoirs in this manner. Through the water sampling programs, he has noticed that the watersheds, areas above the lakes that have had a lot of cotton grown in them, have a higher concentration of arsenic than those that are mostly range or pasture. Since arsenic is a natural element, it has a long life and the effects on the water supply are long lasting. The EPA is just now developing criteria for arsenic levels in drinking water. It can be removed, but it takes additional effort and additional costs so water rates would go up.

You need only read the ingredient labels for the shock of your life. Even our water is chlorinated and treated with fluoride. Some ingredients are the same chemicals utilized as rubber preservatives and herbicides. Many pet foods and foods we consume are preserved with toxic chemicals.

There is no one looking out for your well being and health other than yourself. The medical establishment and pharmaceutical companies treat our animals as well as humans alike with chemicals.

In 1991 the Texas State Soil and Water Conservation Board, estimated pesticide use to be 3,807,143 pounds. Nearly four million pounds and this from agriculture use only. When you factor in the constant use of chemicals in the cities and homes, this poisoning of our environment is staggering. Consider this, the next time you are waiting for a train to pass, count 25 of those large cars carrying coal, that's 4 million pounds.

It appears the almighty dollar is more important than any humans' or animals' life. I have concluded that the U.S. has no real desire to cure Cancer. Think about it, entire hospitals would close, research laboratories, medical schools, chemical and pharmaceutical companies would go out of business and the resultant loss of jobs is endless. *Death and sickness is a thriving business in this country.*

At the time this book went to press our government has threatened to eliminate the labeling of "All Natural" grains. This labeling is the only means available to assist us in purchasing all natural foods. This is the only way we know if our wheat, corn and other crops are pesticide-herbicide free. This reinforces my belief that our health is really not a primary concern of our watchdog groups.

The September 1996 issue of <u>Scientific American</u> reports an estimate of "1,118,100 new cases of Cancer in the past year." This only covers the 12 major cancers. Approaching the 21st century it appears this country desperately needs help from our elected officials such as government leaders, university professors, and C.E.O.'s. I would ask these ladies and gentlemen to go back to school and obtain PH.D.'s in *common sense* and discard those in political science and liberal arts. Political correctness now precedes morality, ethics and doing the right thing. It is up to you and I to change this system before it is too late. We desparately need *all new congressional leaders* and members such as farmers and ordinary business people with no "Political Agendas".

Public pressure can force companies to eliminate chemicals from pet food and the food we eat. The first step is to read the ingredients label and choose only the chemical free foods for both our pets and ourselves.

Two major pet food companies have utilized Crockett Kennels and my English Setters for research and development of **all natural pet foods.** My knowledge and belief in *All Natural* products was reinforced while inspecting facilities where all natural pet foods were being produced.

While attending a pet food seminar in Minneapolis, Minnesota I met an Alaskan Malamute who had been fed a chemically preserved food his two years of life. His food was changed to an all natural diet. During the middle of winter this animal completely shed his long winter coat. This detoxification process known as "Gluco Neo Genesis" is similar to what occurs with an institutionalized alcoholic or drug addict.

An animal may go off his food a few days or a week; his coat may dull or begin to shed. He may become lethargic. His system has put itself into a state of suspension while it rids itself of the accumulated buildup of toxins. The harmful effects of chemicals are obviously manifested by these symptoms.

Chemical preservatives such as BHA/BHT and ETHOXQUIN are used for one reason. They are cheaper than all natural preservatives and they provide a minimum shelf life of two years. That's right; the food you fed your pet this morning was probably preserved with a toxic chemical and may be two years old.

GASOLINE   50 CENTS A GALLON

You pull in driving your favorite car. While you are waiting in line, you notice a disclaimer sign: "Warning: this gas contains water and chemicals that will harm your engine." Still gonna fill'er up?

This same scenario occurs each time you purchase pet food. You need only read the contents label to find out what's in these products that may endanger your pet.

Many humans abuse their use of alcohol, resulting in cirrhosis of the liver. This disease is fatal without a liver transplant. Alcohol is a chemical and must be processed and disposed of by the liver. Animals cannot have liver transplants. Once this organ is destroyed, the animal dies.

You may be poisoning your dog or cat, unknowingly, a little each day.

Read those ingredient labels and most importantly, read the "Warning Labels". They are there for our information and remember we are the only ones our pets have to rely on.

Remember, chemicals break down the immune system. One problem may be fixed while another part of the body is adversely affected. Sometimes this is apparent and sometimes not. An example of this is hearing loss and balance problems now associated with mycin drugs. Alternatives to chemicals are available. They may be less convenient and more costly; however, they pose no threat to the health and well being of animals and humans alike. Previously Vitamin E, a natural replacement for chemical preservatives, was mentioned. There are two other chemical substitutes that you should be aware of as a pet owner.

The number one killer of dogs is automobiles; the number two killer is kidney disease; number 3 is heart disease; and number four is liver disease. These diseases can be minimized by feeding a chemical free, all natural diet.

Diatomaceous Earth,
A Chemical Replacement

There are alternatives to the chemicals in roach hotels and other pesticides that are used daily. One of these is "diatomaceous earth." I have used it extensively with positive results. Not only does it eliminate unwanted pests such as ticks and fleas, fire ants, roaches; it is actually beneficial to our animals.

Millions of years ago in all the waters of the earth, microscopic, one-celled plants called "diatoms" took the minerals from the waters and created protective shells for themselves. They lived in large quantities beyond the mind's ability to comprehend, and as they died and their shells drifted to the bottom of the sea beds, vast deposits were laid down.

Throughout the history of man's existence, uses have been found for "diatomaceous earth or D.E.," as the deposits were called, and today there are over 1000 ways for man to benefit from this material. Many varieties of diatoms exist. In any particular deposit there can be unique characteristics. In the case of non-toxic insecticide, certain characteristics make it possible for us to kill insects without harming animals, plants, or people. These rare deposits furnish a material that has two very important characteristics: (1) when it is fractured, the particle edges are very sharp, (2) each tiny particle has the ability to absorb liquid.

HOW DOES IT KILL? Insects are not built like higher forms of life. They do not have blood vessels, only a body cavity that holds their body fluids. If they lose as much as 10% of these fluids, they die. D.E. helps them lose the vital 10% or more. How?

Most insects have a "waxy" coating on the outside of their shell. The shell is made of porous material and would allow the body fluids to seep out without the waxy coating. D.E. removes the waxy coating and actually absorbs liquid, speeding up the time of the insect's death. The process is actually more complicated than it sounds, but it kills bugs without endangering animals, plants, or people.

Chemicals and poisonous materials interfere with bodily processes in a chemical way, causing several problems: In applying the chemicals, the poisons frequently get spread over wide areas, and all living creatures, especially man, are very vulnerable to these poisons. Second, the poisons are *"persistent," meaning long-lasting;* and as animals, birds, or fish eat the poisoned insect, or if they come in contact with insecticide because of the "wide-area" spraying, the chemical enters the food chain and is passed on to other living creatures, including mankind. Third, insects have an infinite ability to alter their genetic structure quickly. No insect variety has ever, nor will ever, be wiped out by the use of chemicals. They are able to become immune to any poison and within a few generations cannot be killed with a given chemical.

Since 1940, we have increased the use of chemical insecticides by millions of tons, yet have far more insect problems than ever before. Not only do the chemical insecticides fail to solve the problems, but also they create far worse problems. The increase in cancer, hepatitis, mental retardation, and many other diseases may well be caused in part by the wide use of poisons which we cannot see, taste, or smell. The use of D.E. as an insecticide will tend to eliminate those problems, and since the "killing" process is "mechanical" rather than chemical, the insect cannot become immune and cannot pass on any immunity.

D.E. has many uses for our animals. Fleas, ticks, ants, and roaches which cause misery for our pets can be safely controlled through use of D.E. Pets can have D.E. rubbed into their coat; however, this may give an effect of dryness. It removes the natural oil from the hair, but is only temporary and will clear up after the animal is bathed.

In my outside dog pens, I sprinkle a handful of D.E. into cedar shavings for each dog house. This keeps the house and animal free of fleas. In my kennel area I spread D.E. both inside and outside to eliminate roaches and other crawling insects. I have personally conducted my own research with ticks. It takes up to three days to kill a large tick, but it does kill them. I apply a generous amount around fire ant hills and within a few days the ants die. Many other uses are documented.

Back in the dim reaches of time, many peoples knew of the value of D.E. as an additive to animal foods. In fact, some vitamin companies today use D.E. as a source of trace minerals in their products. Some toothpastes use it as an abrasive to help clean the teeth. There are 14 trace minerals in D.E., and the Dept of Agriculture and the FDA allow the product to be sold as a food additive for animals for up to 2% of their diet.

The Congressional Record, the official publication of Congress has printed a statement that D.E. has a "NO TOLERANCE REQUIREMENT." All poisons have limits as to how much can be allowed into any food materials, but not D.E. I know of no other insecticide that has this allowance.

AUTOMOTIVE ANTIFREEZE—A KILLER

Let me present you with a scenario that occurred. Two gentlemen were ending their day of quail hunting in the South Texas heat of early fall. Their dogs have beat them to the truck. On arrival they find one dog under the truck digging a hole to lie in and cool himself. On arrival home they notice this dog is very lethargic and off his food. They take him to their vet where tests reveal his kidneys had stopped functioning. After a few days and extensive treatment, the dog was dead.

What happened was that while the dog was digging that hole under the truck, he had found a stream of leaking anti-freeze. Because it tasted sweet and cool, he drank all he could. This potential hazard can now be eliminated. A new anti-freeze named Sierra is now available. It is Pet-Safe with no ethylene glycol.

A new study reveals that over 100,000 pets are poisoned each year by automotive antifreeze. Conventional antifreeze contains ethylene glycol which can be deadly to small animals. As little as one teaspoon full can kill a cat, and two ounces can cause the death of a dog. This study was performed by Bruno and Ridgway Associates, on behalf of Safe Brands Corporation and American Society for the Prevention of Cruelty to Animals (ASPCA).

The numbers cited in the study reflect only pets that have been brought to veterinarians' attention during 1996. Unknown numbers of others, as well as wildlife, presumably also have been subjected to the effects of ethylene glycol. The chemical attacks the kidneys, forming crystals and causing permanent kidney damage or death. Veterinarians report that symptoms of antifreeze poisoning include loss of appetite, unquenchable thirst and a stumbling gait. By the time symptoms appear, it is often too late to save the animal.

Three out of four veterinarians surveyed said they had treated dogs and cats poisoned by antifreeze within the past 12 months. The average number of antifreeze poisonings reported per vet is 4.7. The report indicates that 77 percent of antifreeze poisoning result in the pets' death. Antifreeze is estimated to account for about one in four (23 percent) accidental poisonings of dogs and cats. In the United States 3,209 human poisonings were related to automotive ethylene glycol. There were 713 poisonings reported in children under six. A total of eight deaths were listed by the report directly attributable to ethylene glycol.

Sierra Antifreeze is Pet-Safe. It contains Propylene Glycol which metabolizes to a substance which human and animal bodies can process. This product provides performance comparable to premium brands of ethylene glycol coolant. It is our responsibility to eliminate these lethal chemicals, making our environment a safer place for animals and humans.

Remember chemicals remain in our soil and water indefinitely, possibly forever. Let's stop killing our planet unnecessarily.

Chapter Six

THOSE INCREDIBLE CATS & THE SUPERNATURAL POWERS OF HEALING

Middy Kitty

Solitary, independent, aloof, cunning, and extremely intelligent are our feline friends. My experiences with cats began around 1979. One day a kitten appeared in our hunting camp near Brady, Texas. This tiny black cat with beautiful golden eyes was emaciated and covered with ticks. I removed the ticks and fed this starving kitten. From that day on she became the camp cat; she was called Midnight, the time she first appeared. The landing strip for our light aircraft was adjacent to our camp. Each time I prepared to land, I would fly slowly over the runway making sure it was clear of obstacles, deer, or other animals. After landing and taxiing to camp, there would be Midnight, sitting and waiting for me. She and I became very attached to one another. Seventeen years later I would learn just how close this bond was to be.

My wife and daughter were frequent visitors to the camp and they became very fond of this little black cat. Usually I flew my small Cessna the two hundred plus miles to the camp. Periodically the girls insisted I bring Midnight home for visits, so this tiny black kitty began her flights to Dallas, Texas with me. She was comfortable in the plane from the very beginning. Usually she would lay on top of the instrument panel and look out the windshield. However, after about one hour, she would crawl under my seat. A short time later there would be complaints from my passengers as the horrendous odor of cat poop circulated. Needless to say, Midnight made a name for herself very quickly. Years passed and Midnight became a Dallas resident, and loyal companion to my wife and daughter.

One day when leaving I started my truck and was backing up when I heard a loud pop. I knew immediately I had run over Midnight. I jumped out and ran to the rear of the truck where this tiny kitty lay, her pelvis broken in two. The endorphines had taken control and she let me pick her up gently in a towel. The veterinarian informed me there was really nothing that could be done. Her pelvis was broken in two along the path of her spine. He said if she was intelligent enough, she might survive if put in a dark room with food, water, and a litter box. The secret was quietness and confinement. In three weeks she was up and around. At four weeks after the accident, I watched, to my amazement, as she jumped atop our six foot fence and took a stroll along the top.

There are other ways of healing, without drugs. The power of positive thinking and confidence in those supernatural powers are there just for the asking.

During the late eighties she moved with me to Bowie, Texas to live at Crockett Kennels. During this time period, Middy became the main cat around the kennel, helping me teach the young puppies. They learned to stay out of reach of Middy real quick. She would never hurt them but would arch her back, hiss, spit and smack them on the nose. Just one encounter was all a young puppy wanted. During this time period there were many customers who visited the kennel. Middy had the habit of crawling into their car if a window or door was left open. Often she would curl up under the seat and leave with the customer. On many occasions they would return after a few miles, discovering an unwanted stow-away.

During April of 1994 two customers visited, one from Kansas and one from Dallas, Texas. A friend of mine from Fort Worth was here for a day also. During this month Midnight disappeared. I searched everywhere with no trace whatsoever. Months went by as I looked for her next door on the 700 acres where I trained dogs. Nothing! I finally decided the coyotes had killed her while on one of her hunting trips.

Two full years passed when one day I came into the garage. Located next to the back door of the house in the garage was a file cabinet cluttered with spray bottles, paint cans, etc. These were all laying on the floor. I thought this a bit unusual but picked them up and replaced them as they were. I assumed one of the three dogs who slept in the garage had jumped up and knocked them down.

The next morning I left through the back door and noticed the cans and bottles on the floor again. I sat down on the step to put on my boots when I felt the presence of something. I slowly turned, and there on top of the file cabinet was Midnight.

I was literally in a state of shock, not believing my eyes. I then said "Middy, is that you?" and she jumped into my lap and began loving and rubbing on me. Tears of joy began dropping on my cheeks; this was truly a God-send for me and my family.

She had been injured in her journey from who knows where. X-rays revealed a leg had been broken and healed and some vertebra had been separated at the base of her tail. Obviously she had sustained a blow to this area. She could not control her bladder or bowels. X-rays also revealed the old pelvis injury. Today she lives on at the kennels, still helping me with those puppies. She is always at my side when I am at the kennels.

A television station learned of Middy's plight and came to film her story. The film crew wanted close ups of her in the film. They laid the camera down with it on and running. Middy walked up, peered into the camera lens and began chewing the lens ring and later the microphone rubber protector. They got their wish for close ups which were used throughout the thirty minute news broadcast.

John & Middy

Butter Scotch

Another kitten appeared and grew up at the Brady camp. His name was Butterscotch because of his coloration. Butter, as he was called, began to go along on hunting trips, always a few yards behind me. He had this habit, after about 10 minutes of walking, he would began meowing real loud and wouldn't shut up until I picked him up and placed him in the game bag of my jacket. There he would ride for 10-15 minutes with his head protruding. He would then jump out and walk for 10-15 minutes. Then the whole cycle would begin anew; my companions always got a charge out of Butter and his antics.

Bobby cat

An employee gave me a Manx kitten who
very much resembled a Bob-Cat; therefore, I
named him Bobby. He grew to a large size of 14
pounds and was more dog than cat probably
because he grew up with dogs because there
were no cats around at that time. Bobby became
a sidekick, always following me no matter what I
was doing. Next door I would walk the 700 acres
training my gun dogs. Some days I would walk
this ranch more than once. Bobby would follow
in my foot-steps every yard I walked. I would
stop to flush a covey of birds and shoot and there
he was, sitting and watching. The interest he
showed in quail hunting never ceased to amaze
me. He loved the snow and would leap from
track to track when I worked dogs after the

white powder had fallen. Later on, he became the father of Tiny Gooney's Kittens, and died shortly thereafter from anti-freeze poisoning. He was a very special cat.

Tiny Gooney

I also have another cat, her name is Tiny Gooney, named because she was the tinniest kitten I had ever seen. She had a habit of crawling into the sleeve of your shirt or blouse and cuddling very close inside where she would sleep. She and one of my setters named Boo became inseparable friends. Boo would let her nurse even though Boo had never been pregnant. Hence the name Gooney for her unusual acts. Late one night I was awakened by a loud cat fight outside. I went out with a gun expecting I knew not what. I could not find the animals. The next morning Tiny was on the porch and one eyeball was totally deflated. I took her to the veterinarian who advised me she had lost the fluid and her vision. He said he could remove the eyeball if I wanted. I decided to let nature take its course...

Six months after this incident the eyeball had totally repaired itself; the fluid that was lost regenerated and her eyesight was restored. There is a slight color difference but she has full vision.

My faith in these **Supernatural Powers of Healing** saved this cat's eye from the doctor's scalpel. We need only the faith and confidence to let nature work its miraculous charm. One of my dearest friends is a highly successful orthopedic surgeon. His advice, "Do everything possible before undergoing any type of surgery."

Tiny with Two Good Eyes

Cats and Their Circadian Rhythm

Cats sleep 18 hours or so every 24 hours; they prefer to sleep during the day and prowl at night, their ancestral nocturnal heritage.
Many cats experience urinary and bladder infections and blockage. After years of testing it has been proven that stress is the cause of many of these illnesses. It has also been proven that if these cats are placed in a dark room for 24 hours with food and water and left undisturbed; 75% recover completely without medical intervention.

My daughter living in California has two of Tiny Gooney and Bobby Cat's offspring. She phoned one day to inform me her boys had urinary blockage and had visited the vet. The doctor, of course, placed the cats on a prescription diet and antibiotics.

I immediately asked her what had taken place in the days preceding this occurrence. She told me that plumbers had been in her house, banging with hammers and tearing out walls. This interruption of their sleep and habit patterns was the culprit.

Remember that many sickness problems in both cats and dogs are directly related to their environment. They feel stress just as humans and often react with various ailments.

The number one killer of cats is automobiles, the number two killer is kidney disease, and number three is liver disease. An **"all natural diet"** will help eliminate premature deaths from kidney and liver disease.

An **"All Natural Diet"** for cats which I recommend and feed is listed below.

Ingredients: Chicken Meal, Ground Yellow Corn, Ground Brown Rice, Corn Gluten Meal, Poultry Fat (Preserved with d-Alpha-Tocopherol and Ascorbyl Palmitate), Whole Wheat Flour, Soybean Meal, Poultry Digest, Lecithn, Dried Cheese, Dried Whey, Brewers Dried Yeast, Calcium Carbonate, Salt, Phosphoric Acid, Taurine,Choline Chloride, Ascorbic Acid (Source of Vitamin C) Vitamin E Supplement, Zinc Amino Acid Chelate, Iron Amino Acid Chelate, Yucca Schidigera Extract, Manganese Amino Acid Chelate, Cobalt Amino Acid Chelate, Calcium Carbonate, Vitamin A Acetate, Calcium Iodate, Niacin, Pyridoxine Hydrochloride (B6), Thiamine Mononitrate (B1), Vitamin B12 Supplement, Vitamin D3 Supplement, DL-Methionine, Copper Amino Acid Chelate, Menadione Sodium Bisulfite Complex (Source of Vitamin K Activity), Biotin, L-Lysine, Riboflavin Supplement, Folic Acid.

Protein	30%(Min)
Fat	16%(Min)
Fiber	3%(Max)
Moisture	10%(Max)
Ash	5.20%(Max)
Magnesium (MG)	0.12% (Max)
Calcium (Ca)	1.10% (Min)
Phosphorus (P)	0.85%(Min)

There is one exception to this recommended diet. Male cats, particularly neutered males should be fed low magnesium (.10% or less) to avoid urinary problems.

I was raised like most youngsters with the belief that if you get sick you go to the doctor. After marrying Janet, I learned of her deep faith in the Christian Science doctrine of healing through prayer and positive thinking. This new found belief began to take effect soon after our marriage. Cats and dogs with serious ailments and injuries, became self-healed because we had the faith to believe in them.

Tony

While writing this book my Paint Tennessee
Walking horse Tony was seriously injured. While
tied up eating the same way he had for the past
year, he became entangled in his lead rope and
fell onto his side. The rope wrapped around his
rear leg just above the hoof. I found him immobilized on the ground, his rear foot swollen

twice the normal size and bleeding from the rope cut. After releasing him, he was very lame and very reluctant to move around. I ran cold water over the injured foot for thirty minutes and doctored the cut with a natural ointment and wrapped the foot and leg for support. I then isolated him in a small pen. (This all occurred while I was called to the telephone and out of view of the horse eating).

Janet arrived home and I related the incident to her. I thought I should call the vet (a natural reaction from my past). She reminded me to give him some time and to think positive. That night this beautiful Paint horse, with his four white feet was in my prayers. The following day I unwrapped the foot and, to my surprise, the swelling was nearly gone. There was no noticeable lameness. Again I ran cold water over the injured area for thirty minutes. (The therapeutic action of cold water is very effective, just as the whirlpool that athletes use). I again wrapped the area for support and by the third day there was no sign of injury other than the abrasions.

A specific religious belief is not required for everyone to witness these incredible powers. You need only believe in yourself and have faith in the animals ability to heal. Prayer is certainly a big part of the overall picture. **Prayer is Positive Thinking**; it focuses our mind on the problem at hand and enables us to deal with the reality of healing and, in some instances, death.

Many years ago I learned about the power of the mind while taking a course in "Instinct Shooting." A gentleman in Fort Worth, Texas was world renown for his school on shooting. I wanted the ability to shoot a can out of mid air like the cowboys on T.V.

My first lesson in *"Instinct Shooting"* was not with a gun, nor was the second. These classes dealt with my mind set and the de-programming of my conscious mind, allowing my sub-conscious to perform. I learned quickly the brain has the ability to calculate what is necessary to shoot an object whether it be in motion or stationary. The secret lies in allowing the mind to perform its magical powers without intervention. I learned the instant the pistol, shotgun, or even a BB gun was pointed, I pulled the trigger. After a week of this, it was common to score 90-95%. This ability is within all of us; we need only the patience and confidence to allow it to work.

On a spring day in the mid-eighties my good friend Tom Misfeldt and I were on a turkey hunt at our camp in Brady, Texas. Crawling through the mesquite thickets we had enticed several gobblers to "talk turkey" to us, but none approached close enough for a turkey dinner. Around mid-morning we were walking back to camp crossing the lake dam adjacent to camp. This dam was constructed with huge boulders on each side of the earthen center.

Tom was walking approximately 10-15

feet behind me, suddenly there was an enormous "Bang" and something hit me in the back. I felt my overalls and there was bloody particles everywhere. I thought I had been shot. Tom was kneeling on the ground and then I saw it, the remains of a huge Diamondback Rattlesnake! I asked Tom what happened and he was in a state of shock and weak from what had occurred.

He said, "As I walked along the dam, I saw this snake un-coil and strike at your leg. As it did so I 'instinctively' shot the snake." Tom may have saved my life that day. At the very least, he prevented a nasty bite and a trip to the hospital.

Tom, also had taken that course in Instinct Shooting with me.

The Power of Positive Thinking is more powerful than any chemical, drug, physician, or hospital staff.

Chapter Seven

LUCI AND DOG STORIES

My Luci

Luci, She lays here by my feet
For Her, there's no schedule to keep

I must watch her close when going outdoors
There's still much more she wants to explore

Twelve years old; that's "70" for us you know
Luci doesn't understand the words "you can't go"

A brand new truck and her own special seat
"Sheepskin" to sit on; she thinks that's neat

A partner like no one else before
I even go around and open her door

Luci, I hope you live forever
you're one smart dog who understands the word "clever"

Luci

Ladi Dog

Luci was born in Dallas, Texas, January 5, 1985, daughter of Crocketts Lil Ladi and Crocketts Deep Freeze. The day she was born I picked her out; I knew she was the special one for me. From that day forward she has been my closest friend. When I needed someone to talk to, she was always there; she understands what I am telling her. Luci has an understanding of many words: bed, couch, chair, truck, blue truck, car, get in tub, get in the back seat, get in the front seat, sit, stay, lay down, come, heel, O.K., fetch, cheese. She recognizes even the verbal spelling of the word cheese and she will bark, shake her head, and tap dance until cheese is served. She understands the word TeeTee and will promptly urinate when told to do so.

When traveling together I often stop for gas, lunch, etc. Each time I return and get into the truck, Luci will smell my breath to see if I have eaten. If so I had best have a "to go" box with her name on it; otherwise she will lay down, look the other way for hours, pouting.

When just six months of age, Luci was in the field hunting with me. On our bird lease near Brady, Texas, she immediately showed her ability to recognize and understand what I wanted her to do. Running in the field, she would stop and look for me and wait until I pointed which way I wanted her to work. My friend and hunting companion, Tom Misfeldt, would just shake his head in disbelief. Most dogs would require two years of training to handle as she did at six months. Finding the scent of quail and pointing them was her specialty. She would not only point but hold the birds for me to flush. Remember she did all this naturally; she had never had any formal training whatsoever. At this time I had instructed my companions not to shoot directly over her head. Although she was accustomed to the sound of gunshots, she was too young to be shot over. On one occasion she pointed and, before I could get to her, a friend of mine shot directly over her head. This literally scared her to death and she ran to me, cowering between my legs. I now had a gun shy dog, one of the most difficult problems to over-come in a bird dog. I felt she could overcome this; so, with the help of my wife and daughter, we began the process. This basically involved taking her food away for a few days. When she became real hungry and eager to eat, her food was placed in front of her. While she ate, with her head down, a muffled blank pistol was fired some distance away. This was repeated at each feeding time. Two weeks went by before Luci forgot the incident and the gunshot became an every day occurrence at meal time.

Back to the field, we were once again enjoying the wonderful sport of quail hunting. I now allowed no one to shoot when accompanying Luci and I in the field.

Approximately three months passed and Luci was improving with each outing. We were at our camp which was situated on a large lake. I was inside preparing lunch for several friends when I heard shots ringing out from an automatic rifle. I ran out the door and Luci was running towards me, terribly frightened. A friend had decided to shoot turtles from the lake bank and Luci had been sitting beside him. Now the process had to be repeated, for Luci was once again gun shy.

This time it was not so simple. She would go for as long as 10 days without touching her food. She knew there would be a gunshot when she took a bite. Needless to say, my wife and daughter were about to disown me for what I was putting this young dog through. However, when I had to leave for several days, they helped and continued the process. Six weeks later she was eating and letting me shoot over her, thanks to her and my family.

These two unpleasant experiences destroyed Luci's beautiful style on point. She would now point with her tail level at the three o'clock position or even between her legs. Her desire to hunt and find birds never faltered. This was no average dog. Some will overcome the first bad experience, but I have known of none who overcame two incidents such as this. To this day Luci remembers the man who shot that rifle. Each time he was around, Luci would utter a low growl and constantly watch his movements. She never made friends with him although he tried each time he saw her.

I force broke Luci to retrieve. She completed the course in 10 days. Most dogs average 45 days. She and Hank are the most intelligent dogs I have ever known; their desire to please is incredible.

Luci and I have shared a special friendship for the past 12 years; a relationship of a best friend, that I can't adequately explain, just experienced. Her days are numbered and I am preparing for the time she departs this life for another. I have been blessed with her companionship and love. These feelings will last forever after she passes on.

Luci and Bobby Cat

Luci had six littermates at birth. One of them, Bandit has lived with me all but two of his years. A third littermate, Chloe lives with my friends, the Misfeldts.These three have been fed **All Natural** foods their entire life and never been ill. The fourth was killed by an automobile, and the remaining three all died of cancer before reaching the age of nine. All three of these dogs were fed *chemically preserved foods*.

Smooth Move
"Checkers"

Checkers is a very unusual dog. She has attained First Place wins in four different types of field trials. Two of these are Walking Field Trials and two are Horseback Trials. She has the unusual ability to do both. In January of 1995, I had her checked for pregnancy by both X-Ray and by palpation. Both were negative with no sign of puppies at 35 days after conceiving. The normal gestation period is 62 days for dogs. At the 50th day of this term, Checkers competed in a trial on the coast of Texas. This was a qualifier for the NBHA National Championship. She put forth an extreme effort and was flawless. She was awarded first place and a trip to the Nationals. During her last 10 minutes of competition I noticed her tiring, unusual for Checkers. She has always been an easy keeper with energy to spare. I returned home and 11 days later she was dripping milk and acting very pregnant. I drove her to the vet who examined her and there was one huge puppy waiting his chance to appear. She began labor and only two feet would emerge. He was too big to slide pass the cervix. A cesarean was performed and Lucky pup arrived. Due to Checkers incredible physical condition, we decided to allow the pup only one week to nurse and then bottle feed him. I would then have eight days to prepare Checkers for the national competition. She was roaded a few minutes to begin with and increased a little more each day. She went to Tennessee and gave a good performance, still going strong after her one hour race. She won her last trial in 1995 at 11 years of age and was retired.

Checkers and Luci have always been best of friends, both traveling together. Luci has always had a *prima donna* attitude towards other dogs. She has only befriended two dogs, Hank and Checkers. She and Checkers always ride up front in the truck with me, very seldom in back in dog boxes. These two always stay in the hotel room. The one time I made Checkers spend the night in the trailer, she competed the next day at a field trial and promptly caught a bird and ate it. Field Trials are designed to watch bird dogs *point birds*, eating one disqualifies the dog instantly. This was the only time I ever saw her do this. This was her way of telling me she was not accustom to overnighting in dog crates and would not allow it in the future. From that day on I didn't abuse her ego and she didn't embarrass me again.

I admit to keeping dogs in hotels, sometimes when I shouldn't. I was in Oklahoma for a trial and stayed at a new Holiday Inn. I was on the fourth floor and would enter via the rear stairs. I didn't know whether I was supposed to have dogs in the room or not and didn't ask; therefore, I was trying to be discreet. One evening I climbed the stairs with both dogs behind me, and once in the hallway, I walked briskly to my room, some 12 doors down. Usually Luci and Checkers beat me to the door and were waiting. This time they were not. I put the key in and opened the door, looked around and no dogs were to be found. I called their names quietly; still no Luci or Checkers. By now I am becoming more than a little concerned; I began walking back up the hall gently calling them and then they appeared. The doorways were all recessed and there were these two heads peering out from one of the entry ways, Luci with a half eaten grilled cheese, and Checkers with roast beef. They had stopped in to snack on someone's room service.

I cracked up with laughter. What a twosome— partners in crime!

Chelsea

My family has been filled with women, no boys. In the sixties while flying for Delta Air Lines I moved to Dallas, Texas. Just up the street were high school classmates of mine from Kentucky, Jack and Nancy Zogg. They had a son who became the closest thing to a son I would have. Our relationship is a life long story of travels, fishing, hunting, and camradery.

A small Golden Retriever puppy came into the Zogg family, and things have not been the same since. Chelsea went everywhere with John and I. She was a Gold Medallion Flyer in the small Cessna. This was a very unusual puppy.

She loved the report of a gun and began looking for something to retrieve at the sound. She proved to have the desire and determination of a Champion. It is unbelievable, but at four months old she would sit with John at the edge of a pond and retrieve the ducks and doves he would down. She would get so tired she would bring him the bird, crawl under his seat and go to sleep. "Bang," the gun would go off and she was in the water looking for another bird. John didn't miss often. When he did, she would just keep on swimming and looking at John for directions. She was his greatest critic on how not to miss. She is the only retriever puppy I have known of who was retrieving in the field at that age.

Chelsea & John

During the 1980's I often hunted waterfowl at a camp located along the Red River, north of Honey Grove, Texas. A deserted house had been refurbished for our camp. John and I often hunted together with Chelsea and my Labrador, Tillie. It was during one of these extended trips that a very unusual incident occurred. Chelsea slept with John and Tillie with me.

Mandy & Tillie, Mother & Daughter

We had cooked a rather large meal with a 25 pound turkey and the group had dined together for the evening dinner. We were in bed early as we were usually up by 4:30 am. The turkey had been left on the kitchen table, partially eaten, with plenty left for another meal or two. The next morning at breakfast there sat the remains of the turkey, still on the table and on the plate exactly as it was the night before, but only the breast bone remained! Chelsea and Tillie had conspired during the night to have a turkey dinner. The amazing part of this story is there was absolutely no mess and no sign the dogs had been there. The telltale signs of diarrhea clearly implicated the two. I can only imagine the sight of the two of them standing on their hind legs, with their paws on the table eating that turkey from each side. How they kept from making a mess while leaving the remains intact is still a mystery.

Chelsea and Luci, both the same age, are more than just dogs, they are members of these two families.

Best Firends

My daughter Stephanie was two years old when I purchased Cricket, a miniature screwtail Boston Terrier. From the beginning the two of them were inseparable, with Cricket sleeping in bed with Stephanie between her legs under the covers. She was extremly protective and she always barked at the mailman, Richard. She hated him for some unknown reason. He was always trying to make friends with this little nine pound dog. Cricket was never interested in his gestures of friendship. At this time we were living in the city of Dallas, Texas. One day I was in the back yard when I heard someone shouting from the front yard. I walked around the house and found the most hilarious sight I had ever seen. Cricket had treed Richard the mailman in the fork of a large Mimosa tree. Richard was throwing mail from his mailbag at Cricket and the ground was littered with the neighborhood mail. Cricket was furious, growling and barking. What a sight, a nine pound dog forcing this man up a tree. I finally intervened and picked up Cricket as Richard descended the tree. I apologized and we both had a good laugh while picking up mail.

Pals
Cricket & Midnight

Field Trials

Field trials provide an accurate evaluation of a dog's overall performance. They are the proving grounds that afford an opportunity to assess the animal's desire and intensity and scenting ability to correctly locate game. An all important aspect of these trials is the dogs rapport with his handler and his desire to please. This in itself is indicative of the trust and intelligence of the dog. I would consider the improvement of the breed the foremost purpose of field trials. The dog that wins the major championships does so with ability more often than luck. There are many types of field trials: trials for Hounds, Retrievers, Spaniels, and the Herding dogs. The one I am most familiar with is for the Pointing breeds, specifically for the English Setter, English Pointer, German Shorthair, and Brittany.

The dogs who win the major championships often become the cornerstones of the future. They are bred extensively and their genes are passed on for many generations to come.

The pointing dog trials began in 1866 near Stafford, England. In 1874 the first trial was held in the United States near Memphis, Tennessee. The first National Championship was held in 1896, won by an English Setter named Count

Gladstone IV.

Typically a professional trainer would begin his year in Canada or Northernmost states where many trainers have summer training camps. Field Trials begin there in August and proceed south and eastward, with trials in North and South Dakotas, Wisconsin, Kansas, Oklahoma, Mississippi, Alabama, and other states ending up in Tennessee in February for the National Championship.

Today there are three coveted championships in the bird dog world, sometimes referred to as the triple crown of field trials. First is The National Championship which is run on the Ames Plantation each February near Grand Junction, Tennessee. Secondly, The National Free For All Championship held at the Sedgefields Plantation near Alberta, Alabama. The third is The Quail Invitational Championship held near Paducah, Kentucky.

These trials demand a supreme effort on behalf of the animal. They often run in adverse conditions and require three hours of stamina and endurance. The dog will run approximately thirty miles during one of these three hour events.

There are only two individuals who have won all three of these prestigious championships in the same year. It is my privilege to be friends of both, and I am proud to recognize them: Billy Morton whose wins came in 1971 with the famous English Pointer Champions— Wrapup and

Allure, and Gary Pinalto won in 1995 with Champion Borrowed Money and National Champion Lipan.

Billy has trained dogs beginning when he was eight years old under the tutelage of his father. He has been actively involved in the sport all his life, now over fifty years. Billy won the National Championship two times, The National Free For All Championship eight times, and twice won the Quail Invitational Championship. 1996 marks his 28th year at the Sedgefields Plantation where he actively manages their ongoing wildlife program.

Gary lives in Roxton, Texas when not on the road field trialing. He has professionally trained dogs since 1984. A graduate of Rutgers University with a business degree, Gary found his calling was with animals and the outdoors instead of an office. Often I have visited and worked dogs with him, both at his summer camp in North Dakota and in Texas. His work ethic, dedication and rapport with dogs is the best I have seen.

Both of these men are class individuals, their ability to train and handle field trial dogs is second to none. Their attitudes toward training, a firm but gentle hand, has rewarded them many times through the years.

In the picture below with Billy Morton there is a gentleman in the background I must tell you about. His name is Ben " Man" Rand who scouted for Billy.

Billy Morton and National Champion
Wrapup with
Ben "Man" Rand in background

Scouting is probably the most difficult job in field trials. The individual must be familiar with different dogs and watch them constantly when competing. He must be an excellent horseman, riding at many different trials with varied terrain. Often he is required to scout deep into unfamiliar forests in search of a lost dog. Always he must be aware of his position and surroundings so he can discretely return the dog to the front of the judges.

Ben "Man" Rand is the only Black Man and field trial scout ever enshrined into the Field Trial Hall of Fame. "Man" scouted Eleven National Champions, Seven Natl. Free For All Champions, Three Natl. Derby Champions. It has been said he is the best ever to yard train bird dogs. His secret weapon was "Patience". Today he lives near the Sedgefields Plantation and is somewhere between eighty and one hundred years old, no one knows.

Gary Pinalto with National Champion Lipan
and Champion Borrowed Money

Chapter Eight

HANK, THE AUSTRALIAN SHEPHERD

At Crockett Kennels all our animals are an important part of our family, and this story is about a special Australian Shepherd named Hank. On December 24, 1992, my step-daughter, Andrea, my wife, Janet, and I drove to Decatur, Texas for Christmas Eve dinner. A popular restaurant is found there on the historic courthouse square. As we approached the front door of the restaurant, there sat a little puppy four to five weeks old apparently dropped for someone to pick up. Andrea immediately had him in her arms and asked to keep him. I said we would talk about it over dinner so we put him in the back of the truck. During dinner we all agreed if the pup followed us all the way around the courthouse square, while we Christmas shopped and looked at lights, she could take him home. Each time I looked back there he was at Andrea's feet. He went home with us that December night to become a valued member of our family. Unknown to me at the time, this would be the greatest Christmas gift I would ever take home.

This was the ugliest pup I had ever seen; he looked exactly like a hyena. His color was a mixture of grayish silver and black. He had golden amber eyes, and you could always feel his presence when he was near. Everyone who visited the kennels became enamored with him. From the very beginning, I realized he was no ordinary dog. His level of intelligence was incredible as you will see.

We live five miles from town. Our property has almost a mile of farm to market road frontage, and the house sits a quarter mile from this highway. The kennels are one-half mile back and not visible from the highway. A friend of mine passed away and, out of respect, I purchased his small 1979 Chevy Luv truck. I use it mostly around the ranch and for the short drive to town for supplies. From the first day I brought this truck home, Hank adopted it. It was his truck. He slept in the pickup bed waiting for me to go somewhere. I never went anywhere in that truck without him, except once. I was in a hurry one day and I drove to town forgetting about Hank totally. After a short visit I was on my way home when I saw an animal running up the middle of the highway about three miles from our ranch entrance. I began to slow and then I saw it was Hank. He was on the way to town to find me and "his" blue truck. I stopped and in he jumped giving me a hard look with those eyes of his.

One morning I left the house headed to the kennels and Hank was not around. Thinking he had already gone to the kennels, I looked there. After a few hours I became concerned and started to the highway. Fearing the worse, I stopped by the house to tell Janet. As I was leaving, I looked at the blue truck and there sat Hank, behind the steering wheel looking at me with those beautiful eyes of his. He had crawled in through the rear sliding glass window.

Each time I left the house to walk or ride

the four-wheeler the quarter mile to the kennels, Hank was there waiting. He would walk by my side, or he would race the four wheeler or whatever method of travel I chose. He had amazing speed, and he nearly always won the race.

As I worked my English Setters, he would always watch, never interfering. He would merely lay under the big oak tree and scrutinize every move I made. When I finished, he would always have a ball or something in his mouth for me to throw. He retrieved to hand naturally from the very beginning. When it was hot after playing his games, he would walk to the pond, *DIVE* in and swim for hours.

Rattlesnakes are a constant threat six months a year around our place. They have bitten two dogs and a horse during the past eight years. Each summer I de-snake all the dogs as I did Hank when he was eight months old. I exercise dogs four at a time from the four-wheeler in a sledding type harness. This is called "roading dogs." I am always concerned about snakes; however, Hank would run ten to twenty yards in front of the motorcycle. More than once he stopped and alerted me to the presence of a rattlesnake.

I work dogs off horseback a few miles away on a large 12,000 acre cattle ranch. More often than not when I arrived in the pasture to put out the chain and dogs, a large group of cattle would approach and sometimes walk right in the middle of the dogs. A chain forty feet long is staked to the ground at one end and tied to the front of my truck at the other. Every three feet there is a two foot length of chain where I snap a dog. Usually a total of ten to twelve dogs are on the long line. A cow wandering into the middle of this group of dogs creates a dangerous situation. The dog is trapped and cannot escape a mad mamma cow or bull. So, I began taking Hank, and I would tell him to get the cows away. He would herd the cattle and move them in the direction I would point. One toot on the whistle and he would quit and come back. This was all natural; he was my constant companion and a working helper everywhere I went.

Hank was the guard dog personified. Never mean or aggressive, he would just let a stranger know he was not welcome unless we were there to assure him it was O.K.

During one of my dog workouts, I lost a young pup, appropriately named "Houdini", as he pulled a disappearing act. After searching for hours, there was no sign of the pup, and nightfall was approaching. The following day Hank and I returned. From horseback I began the search with Hank who was always ahead and looking. He knew exactly what we were there for; I knew this for certain. After four hours of crisscrossing and searching the better part of 3000 acres, Hank disappeared. A short time later I found him at the edge of a pond with Houdini at his side.

Australian Shepherds are extremely possessive and protective. An incident occurred displaying this characteristic. Near the kennels is a large oak tree. Around the tree are four stake-outs with ten feet of rope on each. This allows the dogs a twenty foot circle in which to exercise and bask in the morning air and sunshine. By noon the summer heat in Texas is 90 degrees or more, so I put everyone back in the kennel. I had two females and two males staked out. I had unsnapped one female and had her by the collar and was walking over to release a male dog when he began an aggressive bark. Hank thought the male was showing aggression to me and he attacked him, taking him to the ground by his neck. I still had the female with one hand and I walked over to grab Hank by the legs to pull him off of the other dog. As I walked by another male Bandit, a 12 year-old normally totally docile setter, leapt up and bit me on the butt, taking me and the female to the ground. Now I am lying on the ground with a hold on Hank's leg with one hand, still holding the female with the other, and another dog holding onto my rear end! What a mess and no one there to enjoy it but me. I am sure it would have made a funny video. Finally I separated them, doctored my posterior and it was over. To this day I have a scar to remind me of this incident.

Bandit
The Normally Docile Setter

For 25 years I have raised English Setters and Labrador Retrievers. I am a friend to all, but Hank was different. He had no title of a champion. He had no registration papers and was a mutt picked up from a street corner. However, he was the most intelligent, loyal dog friend I have ever known or hope to have. He could interpret exactly what I wanted from him and he never forgot.

On May 28, 1996, he and one of his pals who slept in the garage with him got sick. Janet rushed them to the vet. They had consumed a terribly toxic poison and Hank's kidneys and liver had stopped functioning. He was dead 12

hours later. His buddy, Sammy, survived.
We had Hank autopsied, and while waiting for
the results, we racked our brains and searched
our place for some clue. My local vet said it was
one of the most awesome cases of internal organ
destruction he had seen. Finally, after 10 days
the results came back and, to our amazement, the
toxic chemical was algae poisoning!

Many animals are exposed to this unknown killer. It is ever present in stock tanks
and ponds. In hot weather when coupled with
drought, nature produces an algae bloom. That
greenish-blue scum you see around the edges of
bodies of water is a lethal killer. Several calves
and a cat in my area also died from this algae
intoxication.

However, in our search before we learned
the true killer, we realized that our garages and
homes are full of chemicals, herbicides, and
pesticides. With just a few licks from antifreeze
leaking from a car or a chewed up roach hotel
placed in the corner somewhere, the animal may
die. *Please read the labels; nearly all of them
say "Harmful to Pets"* and are killers. I hope I
have alerted you to some potential dangers. We
all need to do our part and try to eliminate these
chemicals from both human and pet environ-
ments; thereby making our world a safer place
for all.

The medical textbook definitions of "Blue
Green Algae Intoxication" are as follows: "Toxin
producing blue-green algae are a rare cause of

hepatotoxicity and fulminate acute hepatic failure in dogs. Algae proliferate in fresh water ponds, shallow lakes, and lagoons. Dead or dying algae, which form a thick green scum on the water's surface, cause the toxic principle...Toxicity is caused by ingestion of algae contaminated water and is most likely to occur in the summer when the warm water promotes prolific growth of algae. Clinical signs consist of acute vomiting, diarrhea and lethargy..."

Hank

You were never just a dog, but my best friend
Each morning you waited for me,
be it cold or in the hot blowing wind

You loved to race the four wheeler each and every day
And then you'd wait as I washed the kennels,
hoping I would play

I'd find you sitting in your truck, eager for a ride
Off we'd go to town for yogurt, you and Luci and I

You walked the fields with Janet each day
I believe you had a message you often wanted to say

Thanks, Andrea, Janet, and John, for picking me up on
that Christmas Eve,
And giving me a wonderful life before my time to leave

The loyalty of a dog to his master; there is no greater love
Please dear God, give Hank "a special place" in
heaven, with you, Up above.

Daniel Baird with Hank and Luci

Chapter Nine

VETERINARIANS AND HEALTH CARE

Veterinary practice today benefits from a world of high technology. Advanced procedures are available for animals just as they are for ourselves. A local general practice veterinarian should be an integral part of your family of animals. Annual vaccines and a once a year physical are essential. Today there are veterinary specialists you should consult with any serious problems. There are animal ophthalmologists, internists, and dental specialists available in most major cities. In extreme cases take your animal to one of the veterinary medical schools. Their staff is diversified and can handle the most serious of problems.

You wouldn't go to the dentist for an eye exam so give your animal the same consideration. Veterinarians have a difficult job with long hours. Don't expect them to be experts in every field of medicine. These are some of the most dedicated individuals I have known, and they have my respect.

You have probably contracted a winter cold at one time or another. By now you know you will recover in about seven days without taking drugs. On the other hand you can take drugs and still recover in seven days. This analogy is true for many animal problems with one exception. Many maladies affecting animals are human induced as seen in the many examples of poor nutrition. Most owners never read the ingredients label and have no idea what the food contents are; this causes many problems. Secondly, many owners neglect their animals' teeth. The buildup of bacteria causes many infections. Many times the veterinarian is required to treat the owner rather than the animal. There are those who would change doctors if told to take their pet home; he will be O.K. with no treatment. Therefore, the vet often will prescribe some mild drug, antibiotic, etc. to appease the owner.

Veterinarians are experts at dispensing drugs for various problems; however, I know of no veterinarians who are experts in the field of animal nutrition. I have yet to interview just one vet who had any formal training in nutrition. While in vet school, these students are lobbied, you might say, by various companies. Pet foods and animal vaccines are provided while these students are undergoing their education. After they graduate, many continue to use those products with whom they are familiar.

Today many antibiotics which are being dispensed by veterinarians are affecting hearing or balance; some are affecting both. I suggest you stay away from giving your pet any drugs with "mycin" in it.

Most of us believe our dogs are heartworm free because we had the dog checked and give him once a month medication. Wrong; heartworms have built up a resistance to those drugs. Your dog may have heartworms which are sterile and the normal blood test will not reveal their presence. You must have your veterinarian conduct the new antigen test.

There are alternatives for some drugs and chemicals. For many years I have used a vitamin supplement known as Ester C. Miraculous results have occurred in older and arthritic dogs. Also my field trial dogs have benefited with additional endurance and quick recovery from strenuous workouts.

Vitamin C occurs naturally in animals, contrary to humans who must obtain it in the food that is eaten. This vitamin aids in the lubrication process of the various joints in animals. The common form of Vitamin C is ascorbic acid, which often upsets an animal's stomach, and much of its effectiveness is lost in urine excretion. Non-Chelated, over the counter vitamins are only 8-10% absorbed. Chelated products are 40% absorbed. Ester C is a superior form of Vitamin C. Ester C locks in the molecular structure of calcium which the animal's system readily absorbs thereby reaches the cells faster and more effectively.

Since my introduction to Ester C several years ago, I have given large doses (1000 mg - 2000 mg) daily to my older dogs when they hunted. Prior to using this supplement these dogs were stiff and sore after a morning's hunt, even though they were properly conditioned. When given the Ester C, they behaved like youngsters with very little soreness. These ten to thirteen year old gun dogs and field trial dogs clearly showed the positive results of this vitamin supplement.

In the January, 1996 issue of <u>Outdoor Life</u> magazine, an article under "Hunting Dogs" titled "Miracle Cure for Hip Dysplasia," reinforces the positive effects of Ester C.

Mark, the Labrador fifteen years young
Thanks to Ester C

There is another product I recommend, called Adequan. It is a natural derivative extracted from the trachea cartilage of bovines. This product is approved for both horses and canines in Canada. It is only approved for use in horses in the U.S. at this time; however, it is being given to canines. Adequan increases the synovial fluid viscosity in affected joints. I have used this product on several animals along with Ester C with great results.

Micky the Rottweiler

Micky, a 100 pound Rottweiler with hip dysplasia belongs to a friend in Cornersville, Tenn. This dog had problems getting around after laying down for awhile with obvious pain in the hips. After two injections of Adequan and one month of large doses of Ester C this dog now jumps into the back of a pick-up, unassisted. He shows no symptoms of hip dysplasia and is given Ester C daily.

There are a few pet foods on the market with Ester C listed as an ingredient. Read those labels! I assure you, with proper nutrition and exercise, you will seldom need the services of a Veterinarian.

YOU MUST READ THE INGREDIENTS LABEL
AND KNOW WHAT YOU ARE FEEDING YOUR ANIMAL.

Those pet food advertisements on television are just that, paid advertising endorsement. I know I have been in those positions several times. I only endorse those foods which are ALL NATURAL. That eliminates 75% of the foods available.

Luci Modeling dog boots

I developed these dog boots some years back after extensively testing others on the market. At the time I was training dogs along the Red River; the area was infested with grass burrs, lethal weapons to man and dog alike. I designed a boot which the dog could comfortably run in without rubbing his feet raw in a few hours.

The secret to comfort is how you attach them to the dog's paw and the boots being the right size. I use three different sizes of a motor cycle inner tube. I cut a length of 6-8 inches and round one end. I then apply a surgical-type tape to the dog's leg. This tape sticks to itself; not the dog's leg. This allows him freedom with no pulling and irritation when running. I slip the boot over his leg, leaving two inches protruding beyond his toes. I now use black plastic electrical tape to wrap around the boot top and to the surgical tape underneath. Over 1000 pairs of these have been sold with compliments on their usage.

First Aid Kit

I carry a first aid kit for myself and a separate one for the dogs. The dog's kit contains Dextrose or some non-chocolate candy for hypoglycemia, large tweezers and forceps, thermometer, natural tears eye drops, betadine, small baby diapers, adhesive tape and ace bandage, rubber bands, and a fleet enema as well as Benadryl antihistamine tablets for bee and wasp stings. I suggest always carrying an adequate supply of fresh water and ice. These two can save a dog's life and are most important.

Over heating is always a concern with high temperatures; however, heat prostration can occur in climates with temperatures in the seventies if the humidity is high. If you're hot and perspiring, so is the dog. The only difference is that he covers 3-5 miles for every one you walk. He can't talk when he gets too hot; he will lay on his side and gasp for air. Death is imminent unless you act quickly.

This happened to me. The first time I did not act swiftly enough and the dog died in 10 minutes. The second time I was prepared; I wrapped the dog in ice and then I filled the fleet enema with ice water and administered an ice water enema. This is identical to the emergency action a vet will take. The animals core temperature must be lowered quickly or the animal will die. By the time you rush an animal to the vet with heat prostration with no immediate action on your part, he could die.

Do not make him drink as his system has shut down; it is useless and will impair his breathing. Get the animal cool and to a vet quickly so he can receive replacement fluids which are vital to his recovery. Pack the ice around his belly area mostly, not the back. Pouring water or ice over a dog's back is very ineffective at cooling. All the vital organs are contained in the belly, and this is where the water and ice are most efficient and should be applied.

Irreparable damage has taken place when overheating occurs. Blood pressure soars to the point of exploding the small capillaries in his nose. Usually their glucose level drops to a dangerous level. This dog should never run in hot weather again. His heart and vital organs have all been affected by this experience.

The dog's temperature is the best indicator of his health. It should read around 101.5 degrees or slightly lower when resting. For anything significantly lower or higher, seek the advice of the vet and do not work the dog.

My best gun dog, Traveler, was a victim of heat prostration. Today I am very careful when hunting him. Unless I need a jacket on, I do not take him afield even then I watch him closely. When I see him stop under the shade of a tree, I know he is overheating. Sometimes he will stop and begin digging a hole, another warning sign to stop!

Remember these clues when you're afield during warm weather.

Traveler

Bloat

Bloat is a word you seldom hear, but a very serious problem. This condition is similar to "Colic" in horses. Simply put, it is a stomach ache. It occurs due to improper feeding and or watering. A dog's stomach is very small and must be given time to empty after feeding and drinking. I allow a minimum of one hour and more if possible before exercising a dog. Allowing the dog to exercise immediately after eating may cause the stomach to twist, cutting off the blood supply, a serious condition that is often fatal. Again, common sense is the rule. Would you run a marathon immediately after you downed a full meal? Probably not, then don't ask the dog to!

Chapter Ten

TRAINING ANIMALS THE HUMANE WAY

Puppy Love

What I enjoy most is teaching puppies. For these little guys and gals, the first year of their life is their most important period. There should be no negative experiences, just positive ones. Patience and repetition, with emphasis on **Patience**, is the key to successful training of any animal. There is a cardinal rule that should be remembered and followed. **Never Ever** hit a young animal, and never shout or scream at an animal.

Pets are very much like humans with one

exception; their memory and loyalty are everlasting. Just one instance of uncontrolled anger can cause irreparable harm to the relationship between you and your animal.

As a kid, my father taught me to do things right the first time, and I would never have to "fix it." He also told me if I never lied, I wouldn't have to remember what I said. I have tried to live my life and train my animals with those words as my guidance.

A degree as a rocket scientist is not required. A degree in common sense is essential and necessary for properly training a dog, cat, or horse.

Training a house dog, bird dog, a herding dog, or even a horse all require the same repetition of daily practice along with **PATIENCE** and understanding.

Another very important rule to be followed for successful training is always quit when the animal is having fun and eager. Several short lessons are the key to success. Long sessions are tiring and boring; therefore, the animal loses interest. Try and quit when the animal has done well; not after he becomes bored and his mind is elsewhere. There are many books available on training animals. Many different methods are offered. I will touch briefly on those utilized at Crockett Kennels which may be different and unusual.

John and Walter, two days old

Bonding establishes an intimate relationship that lasts forever. I have found this process an important key to successful training. Whenever new animals are born on my ranch, I make sure the first thing they see when they open their eyes, other than their mother, is me. I spend hours each day with new puppies, new foals, and new kittens. My presence is their safety net to a new world of sounds, smells, and feelings. I want all these new experiences to be pleasant ones. Each time I approach these newborns, they are eager to see me. This bonding will remain intact for the rest of their life just as with a son or daughter.

The earlier (within limits) animals are weaned; the greater the bond. This is the simple process of dependency. Also, the mama is usually appreciative.

One of the greatest examples of bonding can be found in an animal from the humane society or dog pound. Most of these animals turn into excellent, loyal pets. They show just how much they appreciate being given a home.

The first year is the most important in an animal's life. At the age of one year, the dog or cat is the equivalent of a six year old child. You can imagine what a child would be like if neglected the first six years with no guidance from parents. My dogs receive 75% of their training in their first year of life. Different breeds of dogs mature mentally at different ages. Females mature quicker than males. Each animal is different just as each human is different. Some learn quickly and some require more patience and time. Any time a problem occurs without a quick solution, quit. Stop the training session, and analyze the problem. Solve it and begin anew the next day. One stupid mistake can push back an animal's training days or even months.

My training techniques are simple. I allow the animals to train themselves as much as possible. Often I use older experienced animals to demonstrate what is expected.

Every time you play with a puppy, which is a dog in his first year of life, he should learn something. I will give you an example of a young puppy's life at Crockett Kennels.

Dinner Time

Each morning and afternoon before I feed my puppies, beginning at six weeks of age, I have a daily routine. As I approach the pen, I begin calling to the pups. Next I open their pen gate and begin walking briskly ahead of them calling them to "come." As they follow me, I blow my whistle with a toot, toot, toot, toot, another signal to come. Now we are at the pond where I get in the water and let the little guys get in at their option. After a couple of days they are all swimming with me with no fear of the water. Next, we are headed back to the pen and, again, I call and blow the whistle. When they arrive in

their pen, dinner is waiting. Now as they are
eating with their heads all down, I shoot a blank
pistol some distance away. Each day I walk
closer to their pen as I shoot. After a week they
don't even notice the sound. Everything that
occurred was fun, short, and enjoyable. They
have begun their learning process to come when
called. They have learned to love the water and
swimming. They now associate the sound of
gunfire with eating; everything has been enjoyable and fun. I also hold them in my arms each
day, loving them and assuring them that they are
the prettiest pups ever. Socialization is most
important during the puppies first year of life.

Swimming lessons

Next I take them for short car rides each week, up front, not in the back. I hold them in my arms as I drive a short distance. After a few rides at this age, car sickness is usually not a problem. If a dog gets carsick, change his riding place. You might consider how it would feel riding in that closed in area and being bounced around yourself. Now you can see things from the animal's perspective. During this time period of the first three to four months, I introduce the puppies to horses. I bring my gentle gelding, Walter, to the pens for the pups to smell and get accustomed to. Later on he will walk with the pups as I head to the pond drawing little attention from the puppies.

Puppies must learn to swim properly just as humans do. A dog that can't properly swim will become almost vertical in the water, slapping the water with his front feet. Many dogs can't properly swim; they just tread water and tire themselves out.

The bird wing is introduced for a few sessions of play. A fly rod is used with 10 feet of line with a bird wing tied on the end of the line. When the wing is flashed around, the pups will show their instinct to point.

After the pups show independence by running where they please, instead of following me, I take them to my exercise pen. A fenced area of one acre provides the pups with a large area to explore, without getting in trouble. Several types of birds land in this area and the pups begin to point and chase the birds. There is also a large plastic kids' swimming pool full of water for the pups to get in and cool off.

At three months the puppies are hooked up to a 2 foot chain connected to a stake flush with the ground. They teach themselves that pulling is not fun; they give to the chain. Soon after, I begin walking them on a lease, teaching them to heel.

Now they are taken to the pigeon house. Approximately 10 feet in front, they are staked out on a chain. The pigeons fly in and out freely and also land just a few feet from the dogs. The birds know exactly where they can walk out of harm's way. The puppy is now seeing, smelling, and pointing without human intervention. This method is excellent for timid animals.

Now I begin their yard training. I use roller "tumbler" pigeons which will always return as long as their home is in sight. These birds can be gently put to sleep by placing their head under one wing and delicately holding them for a minute or so. You can actually feel their respiration slow and the bird will relax. Now carefully lay the bird on the ground. Young birds will lay there for up to ten minutes before waking up. Older birds will require a small stick or rock placed on top of them to get them to stay for long periods of time.

Travelette
Pointing the Bird Wing

I place the sleeping pigeon on the mowed lawn in clear view so the pup can see the bird. With the pup on a twenty foot check cord, I allow him to walk towards the bird into the wind. Now he will see and smell the pigeon, sometimes pointing, sometimes wanting to grab the bird. One bird and I quit. Then the next day I do the same thing with the bird in a different place. If the dog is aggressive and eager, then I change things after three to four days. I now place grass over the pigeon and again walk the dog into the wind allowing him to find the pigeon with his nose, not his eyes. After mastering this method, I begin styling the dogs, stroking his back, dressing his tail to an upright position, and assuring him things are great.

After a few sessions of this, I stop the bird

work. As soon as the young dogs are showing boldness, I take them to my training grounds. Here there are thousands of acres to run on. I start the pups with an older dog showing the way. I follow on horseback and start assessing the dog's potential. If one wants to run, I encourage him; if not, I work him afoot. In both instances I try to have the dog always in front, never behind or wide to the sides. For those who hunt short, I begin planting lots of birds to keep them at the range a foot hunter wants. For those who want to run, I plant only a few birds, working more on his ground pattern and handling. Essentially I allow the dog to determine which he wants to be, a gun dog or a field trial dog.

It's now approaching a year and the pup is handling and I have shot a few birds for him. I now teach him to whoa, utilizing a training table and then the stake and spike collar.

John Crockett & Training Table

Placing the dog on the training table, I restrict his movements with one chain snapped to his collar. I snap another chain around his flank loosely. When I walk off, the dog will try and take a step, tightening both chains. I immediately turn and say "whoa," while raising my hand (in a stop motion). After several sessions, the pup gets the message and will not move. Next I place a leather spike collar over his head.(I file the spikes dull and short). Connected to the spike collar is a 15 foot check cord. Attached to his regular collar is another 15 foot cord snapped to a metal stake. Beginning at the stake, I walk the dog to the end of the check cord (attached to the stake), and as it begins to pull tight, I then keep walking and tighten the check cord in my hands which is attached to the spike collar. I immediately say "whoa" and raise my hand (in the same stop motion). I now have the dog immobilized with two check cords from two directions. I apply pressure very gently. After 4-6 days the dog will allow me to drop the check cord in hand and I can walk around him calling "whoa."

Next I begin taking him for walks with the spike collar on and attached to a leash. As I am teaching him to heel, I will suddenly say "whoa," and he will usually stop and allow me to drop the leash and walk around him reinforcing the "whoa" command. His whoa training is now complete in the yard.

Next we go to the field anticipating wild

birds. This will complete a gun dog's training. Wild birds behave differently, and it will take the youngster some time to learn their ways. Be patient; he will make mistakes but will learn. I always run the young dogs with an older and experienced dog. He will often do a better job of teaching them than I can.

Simple things like potty training a dog are easy if common sense is applied. Make sure a house dog goes to the potty the first time in the yard. He will then want to return to that spot each time to do his business. He must be taken out often when he is still a youngster.

To break a dog from jumping on you, simply place your outstretched hand forward so the dog's nose will bump into your hand. His nose is one of the most sensitive parts of his body. You then have the discretion of allowing him to jump up only when asked to do so. *Common Sense and Patience*, the keys to successful dog training.

The Electric Collar

Very simply, leave the electric collar to the professional who uses them each day. Many dogs have been ruined because of impatient owners shocking their dogs.

Never shock a dog in a dog fight.

Never shock a dog after he has caught something he is not supposed to.

Never Shock a dog if you can't see him.

Never shock a dog when he's scenting game.
Never shock a dog when on point.
Never shock a dog when angry (It's probably not warranted).
Never shock a dog when he is eating or drinking.
Never shock a dog when swimming.
Never shock a dog when tied out.

Desnake Clinic for Dogs

Each year I desnake all the dogs at Crockett Kennels. This has prevented many dogs from being bitten by poisonous snakes. Simply put, I use the electric shock collar and a snake which is staked out in long grass.

Lesson 1. We lead the dog into the wind toward the snake. Usually when the dog smells the snake they are overcome with curiosity and they walk right up to the snake. At this time when the dog sees and smells the snake he is shocked.

Lesson 2. I now get the snake mad and coiled up in the striking position. I lead the dog into the wind, he now sees, smells and hears the snake. When the dog is within a few feet of the snake, I again shock him.

Lesson 3. Usually by now the dog wants nothing to do with the snake; however, I again lead the dog toward the snake and shock him the third time.

I find if a dog is at least one year old, he remembers this for life. Those younger than one year need a refresher course after growing up.

The snake I prefer to use is the King snake. When disturbed into a defensive posture, this snake inflates himself with air. He then exhales the air sounding exactly like a rattle-snake. Sometimes the snake actually strikes the dog; however, there are no fangs and there are no injuries to the dog. The snake is released after the de-snaking is completed. These snakes are a valuable asset because they are immune to the venom of the rattlesnake, his enemy.

Buying a Puppy and Breeding

Always breed to the best field trial champion you can find. These dogs are the finest blood lines available. They have proven to be genetically superior to most. Their intelligence, their stamina and endurance, their ability to locate game, their desire to please and handle, all these traits they will pass down. Only one out of a hundred puppies ever make top notch field trial competitors. The others are what most are looking for, that superior gun dog.

If I had the opportunity to breed to the great thoroughbred, "Secretariat," or the stallion next door with similiar stud fees, I think I would choose the former.

Buy a puppy from a reputable breeder. Ask to see the mother and father. I have found the dam's influence more important than the stud dog. Make sure the parents' hips and eyes are certified free from problems. I suggest not buying puppies from a pet shop. These pups often have many problems that can be avoided. The initial price for a puppy is the smallest part of the total investment. More often than not, you get what you pay for. My puppies begin at $400.00. On the other hand, a year old gun dog sells for $1000.00. I suggest if you want a hunting dog, then buy a gun dog; it is cheaper and the dog has proven himself. With a puppy, there is no guarantee of stardom.

Chapter Eleven

EMERGENCY FIRST AID AND TRAVEL TIPS

Stephanie Rowe ten years old with "a big' en"

Many incidents have occurred which required my immediate attention to save an animal's life. At my home in Texas I am faced with the constant threat of rattlesnakes. Two of my dogs and a horse were bitten. All three survived because of quick treatment in the field and prompt treatment by the vet.

Snake bites are the most dangerous when a dog is bitten on the leg. Facial bites in dogs usually look worse but are seldom fatal. Both my dogs were bitten on the foot. I immediately applied a rubber band tourniquet at the top of the leg, applied an ice pack to the wound, and drove the animal to the vet. I highly recommend this procedure. With a bite to the face, I would

try and keep the dog calm and cool, while taking them to the vet immediately. Do not cut into the wounds; more damage than good will result.
A horse bitten by a poisonous snake is the opposite of a dog. A bite on the facial area requires immediate attention whereas bites on the body are usually not as serious. The venom of most poisonous snakes in the United States affects the fatty tissue in the body. Severe swelling will occur, seldom fatal to the dog bitten on the face. Horses may have their breathing impaired within a short time period if bitten on the face.

Walter, Age 6 - 17 hands tall

When two years old, Walter, my Tennessee Walking horse, was bitten on his face, mid way up between his nose and eyes. He walked from the pasture to the gate where Janet happened to be standing. She noticed the droplets of blood from four puncture wounds. I knew immediately this was a huge rattlesnake that had struck him. I phoned our vet, Dr. Wayne Porter with an emergency call. Swelling began immediately and the vet arrived within thirty minutes. He anesthetized the horse and began operating with wife Janet's help. Two incisions over an inch deep were made across the fang marks. Janet held the wound open while Dr. Porter dug out black pockets of venom. My job was to hold the horse's head up while this all took place. I made the mistake of watching the procedure, and shortly they were treating me after a mild bout of dizzyheadedness. About three teaspoons of this venomous substance was removed. Walter was then sutured and within three days his face was normal. Today, three years later, not even a scar is present to remind me how close I was to losing this great animal. Walter stands 17 hands tall; we call him the gentle giant. Raised from a colt and always around puppies and dogs, he is a valuable member of our family.

Another threat to dogs all over the country is heat prostration. A detailed description of heat prostration is found in Chapter Nine. I consider this the greatest threat in the field because there are few warning signs.

Many animals become sick when traveling. This can often be remedied by using some common sense methods. Any type of travel that would nauseate you will probably make an animal sick. I begin acclimating my puppies as soon as they are weaned. I take them for short drives while laying in my lap. I never throw them in the back where they can't see or get fresh air. I increase the length of trips until they are sitting in the other seat and riding comfortably.

For those extended trips by automobile, I always feed the animal at least 12 hours before departure. This allows time for all food to be digested and eliminated prior to leaving. I only water the dog during the trip; this eliminates upset stomachs and motion sickness. I stop approximately every 6 hours and encourage the dog to urinate if possible. Always stop at roadside parks where other animals have been. The scent encourages them to follow nature's call. The same procedure should be followed when shipping an animal by air cargo with one exception. I walk them until they urinate prior to placing them in the air kennel for shipment. Many animals will be in their kennel for 10 hours of more. This is hard on the animal's kidneys and bladder. I like making them as comfortable as possible on these trips. Having spent thirty years in the cockpit of a major airline, I would not encourage you to ship via air unless it is absolutely necessary. The Humane Society has done a great job of forcing the airlines to be more responsible with live cargo shipments;

however, under ideal circumstances, I would rather not ship via air.

During the past 20 years, two of my horses have had severe cases of the colic. Walter's mother, Celebrity died of sand colic when Walter was only eight months old. Both had several cupfuls of sand and small gravel impacting their intestines. This could have been prevented had I known then what I know now.

Celebrity and Walter, his first day

My local vet advised me to mix Metamucil with their food for three consecutive days a month. Being the skeptic I am, I decided to conduct some research of my own. Our prize mare, Beauty, was about to be bred. For a week I would have her sonogramed each day by the vet. I had a fecal sample tested and there was a couple handfuls of sand in her stools. During the next three days I mixed approximately 4-5 table-spoons of Metamucil in her food each day. Every day I had her tested again. By the third day there was absolutely no sand remaining. Seeing is believing, and this is now a routine part of our horses monthly preventive medicine. Metamucil is a Natural Psyllium fiber from the plantain fleawort.

Trailering horses and changing altitude can cause a horse to colic. Perhaps you have seen what happens to an aerosol container after traveling on the airlines. Often the container will expand from the changes in pressure. The cabin of an airliner is always pressurized after take off and depressurized for landing. Just as when an airliner changes altitudes, a change in altitude for an animal causes gas in the stomach which must escape.   If it does not, it will create a stomach ache for the horse.

A preventive measure that works for me is this: for three days prior to traveling I add a pint of mineral oil to the horses feed. Also, I stop every 4-6 hours and get the horses out and walk them for 10 minutes, always offering them water. Dehydration contributes to the problem.

Occasionally dogs will have an upset stomach. Loose stools and diarrhea are the first signs. These symptoms often cause the loss of live bacteria in the animals intestinal tract. This bacteria is an essential part of digestion. I feed them plain yogurt only, twice daily for three days. I make sure the yogurt contains active cultures, including Acidophilus. Prolonged diarrhea with an abnormal body temperature reguires a veterinarian examination.

Remember: *"An ounce of prevention is worth a pound of cure."*

Chapter Twelve

"TRIBUTE TO THE DOG"

This memorial stands on the city square of the authors hometown, Owensboro, Kentucky

During the late 1800's a trial took place over the death of a dog, Old Drum. The jury deliberated for only a few minutes before ruling a Mr. Hornsby to pay the sum of $50.00 to Mr. Burden, the owner of the dog. Many appeals were filed, but Mr. Burden was finally upheld by the Missouri Supreme Court. This was a special trial because the attorney served in the Missouri legislature and Confederate Congress. After the trial he became a U.S. Senator for 24 years. In the years that followed, the legend of Old Drum grew because there was no stenographer during the dramatic speech. He later would use this speech in campaign literature. The speech got printed in text to be used for school students to recite. It was a favorite elocution piece for young men and women. Then lawyers, in their studies, were reminded about how to win a case without evidence, and the value of a jury plea. Eventually, newspapers around the country began running the piece, and its reputation grew. In time the story of Old Drum and the dramatic monologue touched dog lovers around the world. Finally, in the World War II era, an effort grew to memorialize Old Drum. People sent stones to Missouri from every state, Africa, the Caribbean, Europe, and the Great Wall of China. On Dec. 12, 1947 a monument made of the stones was placed on the creek banks where Old Drum had been found. Imbedded in it were 50 silver dollars, representing Hornsby's payment. Vandals stole the coins and the stones, and the monument fell into disrepair. Eventually, a drive began to establish a statue of Old Drum at the courthouse. Said one contributor, *My dog's not worth a dollar, but I wouldn't take a million bucks for him.* The statue was dedicated Sept. 23, 1958, where it still stands, Old Drum, standing guard for dog lovers everywhere.

It is strange how tenaciously popular memory clings to the bits of eloquence men have uttered, long after their deeds and most of their recorded thoughts are forgotten, or but indefinitely remembered. Whenever and as long as the name of the late Senator Vest of Missouri is mentioned, it will always be associated with his love for a dog.

THE SPEECH

"Gentlemen of the Jury: The best friend a man has in this world may turn against him and become his enemy. His son or daughter he has raised with loving care may prove ungrateful. Those who are nearest and dearest to us, those whom we trust with our happiness and our good name, may become traitors to their faith.

The money a man has, he may lose. It flies away from him, perhaps when he needs it the most.

A man's reputation may be sacrificed in a moment of ill considered action. The people who are prone to fall on their knees to do us honor when success is with us, may be the first to throw the stone of malice when failure settles its cloud upon our heads.

The one absolutely unselfish friend that a man can have in this selfish world, the one that never deserts him, and the one that never proves ungrateful or treacherous, is his dog.

Gentlemen of the Jury: A man's dog stands by him in prosperity and in poverty, in health and in sickness. He will sleep on the cold ground, where wintry winds blow and the snow dives fiercely, if only he may be near his master's side. He will kiss the hand that has no food to offer, he will lick the wounds and sores that come in encounters with the roughness of the world. He guards the sleep of his pauper master as if he were a prince. When all the other friends desert, he remains. When riches take wings and reputation flies to pieces, he is as constant in his love as the sun in its journey through the heavens.

If fortune drives the master forth, an outcast in the world, friendless and homeless, the faithful dog asks no higher privileges than that of accompanying him to guard against danger, to fight against enemies, and when the last scene of all comes, and death takes the master in its embrace, and his body is laid away in the cold ground, no matter if all friends pursue their way, there by his side will the noble dog be found, his head between his paws, his eyes sad but open with watchfulness, faithful and true even to death."

Chapter Thirteen

A Circle Called Life

Christ said the Lion and the lamb will walk together in heaven; this I believe. In order for our circle of life to be complete, we must give more than we take.

A game of chance or maybe hype
This thing we all refer to as life

The future may be grim or it can be bright
Our animals depend on us to choose
what is right

Their life you know is shorter than ours
Our time with them can be counted in hours

There's a lot to be done by you and me
To make their time here the best it can be

A place in heaven is reserved for them I know
Just as the wind will always blow

This circle of life in which we all live
It's our choice to never take more than we give

Convinced through my Christian faith and the after life experiences of others I know, I will reunite with my family, friends, and animals that have preceded me in death. Perhaps these dogs, cats, and horses are angels from above, with a purpose. Many lives have been changed for the handicapped and terminally ill because of animals. The blind and deaf can lead a more productive life through the eyes and ears of their dogs. I consider myself to be the most fortunate man alive. My life has been blessed through my relationship with God's animals. These wonderful creations try and communicate through body language, their eyes, and movements.

Animals can talk to us if only we listen